EXPERT SELLING

EXPERT SELLING

A Blueprint to Accelerate Sales Excellence

SEDRIC HILL

New York

EXPERT SELLING

A Blueprint to Accelerate Sales Excellence

Published in New York, New York, by Morgan James Publishing. Morgan James and The Entrepreneurial Publisher are trademarks of Morgan James, LLC. www.MorganJamesPublishing.com

The Morgan James Speakers Group can bring authors to your live event. For more information or to book an event visit The Morgan James Speakers Group at www.TheMorganJamesSpeakersGroup.com.

Shelfie

A **free** eBook edition is available with the purchase of this print book.

CLEARLY PRINT YOUR NAME ABOVE IN UPPER CASE

Instructions to claim your free eBook edition:
1. Download the Shelfie app for Android or iOS
2. Write your name in **UPPER CASE** above
3. Use the Shelfie app to submit a photo
4. Download your eBook to any device

ISBN 978-1-63047-716-5 paperback
ISBN 978-1-63047-717-2 eBook
Library of Congress Control Number:
2015911996

Cover Design by:
Rachel Lopez
www.r2cdesign.com

Interior Design by:
Bonnie Bushman
The Whole Caboodle Graphic Design

In an effort to support local communities and raise awareness and funds, Morgan James Publishing donates a percentage of all book sales for the life of each book to Habitat for Humanity Peninsula and Greater Williamsburg.

Get involved today, visit
www.MorganJamesBuilds.com

Habitat for Humanity®
Peninsula and
Greater Williamsburg
Building Partner

TABLE OF CONTENTS

PREFACE

Imagine that you are visiting the great city of New York for the first time and someone comes up to you and says, "I'll give you a million bucks if you get into your car and drive to Los Angeles right now, but you can't use a map or any form of driving direction tools." Then, you find out that you must also drive the speed limit and arrive within the same time period as a person using a GPS or street map. After you confirm that you will in fact receive the million bucks, you start to figure out how to get to LA as you drive west. It is daytime, and you orient yourself to the sun to get a general sense of the west direction. You stop and ask a few New Yorkers (good luck with that), "Hey, which highway leads westbound from here?" Hopefully, the information that you're receiving is accurate and useful. In any event, after some trial and error, you end up eventually making it to LA.

Here's a few key questions to consider: Did the trip take longer than it needed to? What was the effect of going the wrong way or taking wrong turns? Last, and most important, how much more stressful was the drive when you weren't 100 percent certain that you were driving on the correct path? This ad-hoc approach is similar to the path that most salespeople experience on their way to sales success. We sort of mosey along in the general direction of chasing sales quotas as we hope to obtain the income and fulfillment we need, but due to the lack of a clear path to success, wrong turns and dead ends make the journey longer, frustrating, and more obscure than it has to be.

Now let's flip the script: Let's say you accepted the challenge to drive from New York City to LA or, more specifically, to the famous Hollywood Bowl arena. But instead of simply driving westbound, you are given a GPS with the Hollywood Bowl address and geo-coordinates already programmed! Obviously, this journey would go much more smoothly *and* you would reach your goal much faster by following the most efficient path possible. Of course that probably would not be worthy of a million-dollar challenge, but you can see where I'm going with this—this book has been designed to serve as your GPS to selling success.

At this point, you're probably saying, "So that was a cool story and all, but what can this book really do for my sales career?" That is a very good and important question. Today's business book market is flooded with "how to" books that proclaim to teach you step by step how to do all kinds of things. But *Expert Selling* is not just another "how to" book. It's a "mind guide" that reveals how to systematically train your brain for expert performance. True sales performance improvement is not based on a single activity or event such as reading a book or attending a training program. It is modeled on a continuum of personal development using the principles of expert performance. This book serves as your blueprint for that journey because it brings into clarity the most influential actions that improve performance and accelerate expertise.

Remember, even though you have a GPS, you still have to get into your car and drive to reach your goals. The good news is that I am committed to being there with you throughout your trip! So fasten your seatbelt, and get ready for an enlightening and fun journey toward achieving *your* success goals.

Introduction
EXPERT SELLING

The magnificent Princess Resort in Bermuda was the scene of the President's Club Annual Sales Conference. The huge ballroom, filled with over 1,000 top sales professionals, buzzed with excitement. Each of the High Honors winners (top achievers for position categories), were announced on stage. As we neared the end of the award presentations, everyone feverishly awaited the announcement of the top honoree. The announcer interrupted the crowd's buzz and said, "Your chairman of the 2000 Sales Leadership Conference (Top Sales Rep of the Year) is . . . Edward Diba!" The auditorium erupted in a thunderous roar as Ed and his wife, Laura, walked on stage to a standing ovation. After a long clapping spell, Ed took the podium and began his remarks. "Now this . . . is a Kodak moment!" he said. Suddenly, he took out a small camera and snapped a picture of the audience. The crowd broke into more loud applause.

After Bermuda, Ed went on to earn several more Sales Rep of the Year awards as well as many High Honors. In fact, over his twenty-five years with Pitney Bowes, he made every President's Club, except one. I've had the pleasure of knowing and learning from Ed for over twenty years. The question he heard most often from peers and management was, "How do you do it?" Notably, the advanced seller, those with several years in the same role, often will ask a similar question: "How do experts become experts?"

Cognitive Skills versus Behavioral Skills

Most people reason that expertise comes from natural talents and decades of experience. Although we all know the elite sellers achieve the highest levels of success, few understand how and why. Hence, the sales training culture tends to gravitate to what they know best: explicit behaviors. As a result, sellers are inundated with an array of behavioral tasks such as learning products, presenting, and closing, to name a few. While these have their place, they're not enough to move the needle for advanced sellers. Along with behavioral activities, much of today's sales training involves various selling methods. Sales methods like solution selling, insight selling, and others, while important for organizations, do little to help the individual reach expertise.

Given this situation, advanced sellers have few good options for improvement. The training they really need does not yet exist. And signing up for what is available is often viewed as a waste of time. In fact, a 2013 American Society for Training and Development (ASTD) study revealed that as salespeople gain more tenure, they engage in less and less training. This raises an important question: Why do advanced sellers stop benefiting from training?

The reason can be explained by what's known in psychology as *arrested development* (**AD**). This form of AD occurs as a result of the perception of necessity. For example, once most people obtain a driver's license, little effort is given toward improving driving skills. Likewise, after a few years of learning a new role, advanced sellers often hit the proverbial wall. I like to refer to this wall as the wall of *good*. Jim Collins, author of the landmark business book *Good to Great*, said it best: "Good is the enemy of great." Many advanced sellers make it to *good*, but few go on to become experts.

In the aftermath of the 2008 recession, many sales forces were downsized, leaving higher revenue goals for the remaining sales reps. As a result, advanced sellers are pressed to upgrade their skills in order to remain productive and effective. *Expert Selling* therefore addresses two central questions of advanced sellers to move them from good to great:

1. "What are the most influential skills needed to achieve success in sales?"
2. And "How can I get these skills without giving up valuable selling time?"

Locating the Windows of Expert Advantage

Many domains such as sports, medicine, and music have made notable gains by adopting expertise research. Moreover, in recent years, researchers have focused much of their work in naturalistic areas that include business and sales. Remarkably, in most all domains, expert performance is marked by cognitive-based skills versus behavioral-based skills. During the research for this book, I was struck by the vast amount of relevant information from brilliant researchers that's available but rarely used in sales. Dr. Gary Klein and Dr. Peter Fadde have been instrumental in presenting research that points to **recognition** and **situation awareness** as chief cognitive skills of naturalistic expertise. Therefore, my aim, in part, is to share these insights with sales professionals and other stakeholders that seek to improve their results.

Central to the advancements made in sports, medicine, and music is pinpointing the "it" most responsible for expertise for that domain. For salespeople, the "it" is recognition—used to influence positive outcomes with customers. In the sales field, we call this form of recognition **connecting**. Hence, *Expert Selling* is about understanding the mind of the expert to move more advanced sellers across the bar of expertise.

For many decades, we've known that effective selling requires good communication. But ***persuasive communication*** (**PC**) is the vehicle that expert sellers use to express connecting skills. So it's not just about *which* skills are required, it's more about how well they're used. To that end, you'll learn how sales experts perform the most critical *ordinary* skills in *extraordinary* ways.

By now, you're probably envisioning a lengthy training program to learn these skills. Most skills workshops can take anywhere from several days to weeks of much needed selling time. Sales expertise, however, derives mostly from ***implicit learning***, which can be done during routine work or anytime using smartphone apps. This brings me to the question of how to improve connecting skills without forfeiting valuable selling time.

Dr. K. Anders Ericsson is among the world's most renowned research experts on … you guessed it—expertise. Ericsson et al. discovered the activity most responsible for expertise is a special type of training called ***deliberate practice***. Although coaches, music teachers, and, more recently, physicians and law students use it as part of their training, adoption in sales has come much slower. With this book, that wait is over. You will be introduced to a systematic learning process featuring deliberate practice, proven to speed expertise.

I am often asked what it takes to be great in selling. While in pursuit of this compelling question, I have been blessed to learn from the most brilliant minds in selling and academia. My goal with this book is simple: to share what I've learned from experts and science to help salespeople move more quickly to the next level. Therefore, I humbly present *Expert Selling* and invite you to begin your journey to excellence.

SECTION 1

EXPERT PERFORMANCE FOUNDATIONS: "HOW THE SAUSAGE GETS MADE"

Chapter 1

CONNECTING
RECOGNITION
AND SITUATION
AWARENESS IN SELLING

A few years ago, I accompanied a sales team member, Kay Robertson, on a presentation at a large-enterprise computer-consulting firm in Los Angeles. During the dialogue, Kay detected that the buyer needed a ROI (return on investment) analysis. The buyer had not said it explicitly, but after being asked what the approval process would be to move forward, he said something like, "Well, we'll need your proposal and then we'll put our internal piece with it, and from there, it should take about a week to turn everything around." Now, on the surface, this sounds like a typical buyer response. But Kay was listening beyond the words and heard something more that helped her avoid a major snag. Promptly she said, "Hey, you know what else I can do? Why don't I include a detailed ROI so you have everything you need to make the best decision?" The customer flashed a big smile and replied, "Thank you. That would be great. Saves me a lot of time!"

Kay was able to secure the $150,000 order within her forecasted timeframe. This order was valued at three times her monthly quota. Two months later, during a follow-up visit with the customer, I asked about the ROI and how it helped with the buying process. The customer explained that it was a major reason the sale was approved so quickly— all purchases of that amount were required to include an internal ROI to justify the cost to Finance. He informed me that Kay's ROI was basically used to meet this business rule. He basically applied the content from Kay's ROI to complete his internal ROI requirement. We were actually shown the twenty-page document, which, in fact, mirrored the information provided by Kay.

This type of intuitive decision making (connecting) can be crucial to selling success because it is proactive versus reactive. For example, what might have happened had the implicit request gone unnoticed? Here are a few less desirable scenarios:

1. The salesperson may never have provided the ROI data and thus become 100 percent dependent on the buyer's internal analysis. The buyer's analysis may or may not have been good enough to pass the standard required for the finance department's approval.

2. The sale may have stalled if the buyer did not follow through on creating his own ROI. At this point, if the seller detects the issue, she may offer to create it or the buyer may request her to do so. But all too often, the sales cycle is prolonged as a result.

3. The sale may have never closed. Many times a sale starts off perfectly, with high buyer interest, but because of the loss of momentum, it can often fizzle.

As this example shows, the seller's decision making plays an integral role in the sale. The takeaway here is that good decision making comes through recognition of the buyer's implicit needs and concerns. Many sellers make the wrong decisions (or no decision when one is needed), as a result of missing key messages. **Primed-recognition** relates to factoring in the recognized message to make the right decisions. These connecting skills are critical to understanding and responding to various selling scenarios.

What Is Selling Intuitively?

Have you ever heard people say, "He just has a knack" or "She really knows how to think on her feet"? There are many factors that are involved with expert sales performance, everything from exceptional product knowledge to skilled negotiating. But when it comes to attaining the highest levels of expert performance, the difference lies within the cognitive (intuitive) actions, namely **connecting**. Novices who give sufficient effort to improve basic skills become journeymen within a short order of time. However, moving from the journeyman (advanced) level of selling to expertise occurs with experience and implicit learning. In this chapter and the next, we will examine two key subskills of connecting—**recognition and situation awareness**—and their role in expert selling performance.

The Science behind Connecting: The RPD Model

Connecting involves cognitive reaction skills that detect, interpret, and respond to the prospect's messages. To better understand sales recognition, we draw from the breakthrough research resulting from the Recognition-Primed Decision-Making (RPD) model. RPD examines how experts make urgent decisions in naturalistic settings. Research scientist and psychologist Gary A. Klein developed RPD to describe how people actually make decisions in natural settings. Many business people have adopted these concepts in an effort to speed up expertise. The model represents the cognitive processes involved with decision makers who evaluate potential solutions by testing them against specific situational elements. RPD includes three primary elements of decision making: matching, diagnosis, and a simulated course of action. It's a blend of intuition and analysis. The pattern matching (recognition) is the intuitive part and mental simulation is the conscious analysis part.

Recognition, the first stage of RPD, involves matching patterns from situations to those already experienced. The second stage, *diagnosis*, focuses on interpreting cues and information. Finally, the *course-of-action* stage relates to evaluating the merits of a potential decision and acting on it. The model groups decision making into three levels:

1. In less complex situations, a person might quickly recognize and implement a decision based on a previous match of knowledge.
2. In other situations where more information is needed, the person will mentally test the solution and choose the first option that can work.
3. In more complex situations where the situation may not be familiar, the person seeks more information and evaluates potential options until the best one is identified. To put it simply, decisions move through the decision stages either automatically or more deliberately depending on the situation and the level of experience.

Beyond the initial recognition stage, the model becomes much more complex and focused on cognitive decision making. Hence, the recognition aspects of RPD is where we center our attention in selling. It is also the most commonly trained part of RPD since it is much easier to reproduce for learning. In the following chapter, "Situation

Selling," we will examine more closely how RPD is applied to common selling situations.

With traditional sales training, the foci centers on **action-oriented** tasks that are executed preemptively. However, **reaction-oriented** tasks have shown to be much stronger contributors in expertise and expert performance. For example, a salesperson's presentation skills are much less effective if he is unable to recognize the needs of the prospect. Notably, although reaction skills have more influence on expertise, the vast majority of sales training is geared toward action skills.

Recognition and intuitive decision making are mostly found in high-stakes domains where decision making has to be very quick and accurate. Examples include the emergency, law enforcement, and firefighting fields. However, selling is marked by dynamic communication interactions that require quick reactions as well. Throughout **persuasive communication** (**PC**), sellers have a very short window of time to detect and respond to the implicit messages that matter. The stakes for noticing these cues grow higher as the sale moves closer to the buying decision. Therefore, closing and negotiating prices and terms represents ideal windows for intuitive decision making.

The Role of Recognition in Expert Sales Performance

For several decades, researchers have sought to discover the specific aspects of performance that separate experts from novices. In so doing, subjects are observed in a laboratory setting for deliberate practice research in sports, music, medical, and other domains. Many studies strongly support the notion that recognition is at the center of the expert advantage. To pinpoint these window locations, researchers use expert/novice methods. For instance, an expert's and a novice's actions are observed when given the same visual and audio data under varying degrees of difficulty. These methods are also used to discover *why* experts display a perceptual advantage. A 2007 study by Dr. Peter Fadde revealed that experts tend to outperform novices in the earliest phases of the simulated tasks.

In sales, expertise is marked by the ability to quickly detect and correctly respond to messages from the buyer. We refer to this skill as *connecting*. During sales interactions, verbal and nonverbal messages flow to the seller, requiring rapid detection, interpreting, and decision making. Since these skills are implicit and fluid, we describe them as intuitive. Fadde, when referring to recognition, calls it "Spidey-sense." Anyone familiar with the comic series can relate to Spider-Man using his special skill to detect trouble before it happens. Therefore, connecting focuses on the implicit cues and message intent of the prospect. Throughout this book, we break down connecting skills using several case stories and examples along with the supporting science.

Experimental Research versus Descriptive Research

The impact of Klein's RPD model, Ericsson's Deliberate Practice, and Fadde's Expert-Based Training are highly regarded within academic circles. But many in the business community assume that all research is the same. We often accept the "based-on-research" claims of sales training gurus without much proof or explanation. It is therefore important to know what type of research people are citing. There are two prominent methods used in psychological research, each of which have different purposes, advantages, and disadvantages. They are *experimental* and *descriptive*.

Descriptive methods aim to describe a snapshot of the market and its environment. It's considered easier to perform than experimental research but is limited in explaining how and why the results occurred. The vast majority of marketing and sales research involves descriptive methods. These surveys, case studies, and statistical analysis reveal *what* is occurring but do little to find out *why* people behave as they do. In addition, most surveys mostly use self-evaluations and self-reported data, which are subject to biases. In many cases where corporate sponsors of these studies have a direct interest in the outcome of a study, critics accuse them of sort of putting the thumb on the scales--manufacturing the need to advance their product or narrative. While descriptive research has merit and a place within the marketplace, salespeople are looking for clear answers on how to move their skills to the next level.

The body of experimental research on the acquisition of expert performance traces back several decades beginning with Adriaan de Groot's pioneering studies of chess expertise in the 1940s. De Groot identified the most critical situations in chess and employed them in controlled laboratory settings. These experimental models have since been adopted and expanded throughout the research community. This includes theories such as the **deliberate practice** and **naturalistic decision making**. Empirical research on expertise relates mainly to lab experiments or observation of subjects within a psychological context.

Experimental research offers insights that expose the elusive expert advantages of expertise. Characteristics of experimental research include causality—specific and individual focused—and empirical design elements. Experimental studies are much more narrowly focused and require more time and effort. As a result, experimental research is widely held as the highest standard by which other research methods are judged. This type of experimental research is central to the sales concepts presented in this book.

Learning Implicitly from Experts

As they say, "You have to think on your feet in sales." While this rings true, the problem is that it only addresses the "what you should do" part of selling. Thus, the "how to do it" part is often left to chance. This sort of **explicit vagueness** is a common error made by novice sales managers. The directive may be specific but the desired behavior is fuzzy. Everyone knows that you have to think on your feet, but people rarely can explain how to do so. Our goal now is to demystify the vagueness of sales recognition and bring into focus the thinking of the selling expert. Figure 1.1 is a conceptual representation of the core cognitive elements of selling expertise.

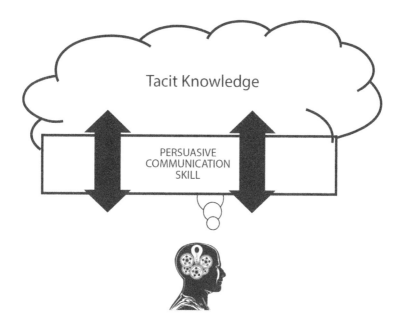

Figure 1.1 Core Cognitive Essentials of Selling Expertise

Many senior managers often ask, "How can we learn more from our top salespeople?" The logical answer is to simply ask the top performers, but experts typically miss up to 70 percent of their implicit processes when teaching a lesser-skilled performer. I learned this the hard way as training director during a major sales conference. I was asked to facilitate a talk-show-style interview panel of the company's top performers. The goal was to uncover best practices that could be later disbursed to the sales force. Armed with a list of well-prepared questions, my goal was to ask the right questions to extract the actions most responsible for their success.

The talks were engaging, and the event went over really well—the audience applauded loudly with cheers at the end of the program. Over the course of the rest of the conference, I talked to many salespeople about the panel activity. Everyone spoke positively about the interviews, but when pressed for specifics of what they took away, the responses were vague and without substance.

This was quite puzzling to me, so later I decided to watch the videotape of the interviews. My questions were in fact well designed and clear. But time after time, the top seller responded with generalized comments. These comments, when analyzed, did not sound much different than what most others would have said.

For weeks, I thought about why the top sellers did not share more useful information about their success. Perhaps they were selfish and did not want to reveal their sales secrets. Or maybe the stage and the lights caused them to freeze up and forget their message. For several more years, I continued to notice how experts struggled to express their knowledge. I eventually learned the reason why. They are simply unaware of much of the ***implicit knowledge*** they use on a daily basis. Perhaps this is the reason many organizations see little impact from best practice activities. Scientist and philosopher Michael Polanyi described tacit knowledge in his work *The Tacit Dimension* as, "You know more than you can tell."

The best way to pull out knowledge from experts is to spend quality time with them. Through these regular interactions, trust grows as the secrets of success are exposed one story at a time. I have been fortunate to have the pleasure of spending this type of quality time with several sales experts including Ed Diba. Likewise, I encourage you to seek to learn and share with other successful sellers to enhance your knowledge. These sharing experiences help to mature intuitive skill by cross pollinating knowledge. Another way to access knowledge from experts is to ask implicit questions. The idea is to ask pointed questions that relate to the expert's thinking rather than her doing. In section three, we will examine in more detail an interrogative question technique designed to unravel tacit knowledge from experts.

The Price of Oblivion

So far, we have looked at the core elements of *intuitive connecting* and the related science that supports it. But what happens when salespeople miss useful cues? It's not that novices completely fail and never make their sales quotas. Of course, many do experience success, mainly early in their sales careers. But once the seller reaches an intermediate skill level, cognitive skills become key in moving to the next level. Failing to improve performance can lead to subpar results and sellers who become stressed and overwhelmed. Other sales metrics can also be negatively affected.

One major reason that many salespeople don't succeed is because of missed cues, a blindness of the sales environment. By blindness, it is meant that the seller will often ignore cues because she doesn't see a reason to react. Others may lack intuitive skills, which leads them to take the path of least resistance. When a prospect sends a useful implicit signal or message, the seller may or may not verbally acknowledge it. But either way, if she is consumed with her own presentation, the opportunity for connecting is often lost.

Pairing up with sales managers or peers on calls is a great way to build connecting skills using reflective learning. The ideal time for a reflective discussion is right after the sales call. The sooner you can talk after ending the call, the more accurate your recall will be. But too many sellers get that rushed, results-obsessed look in their eyes when given the opportunity to receive feedback. As a result, they may miss the reason the sale stalled or why the prospect lost interest. In addition, this situation can be made worse when prospects sugarcoat their concerns.

This happens when the seller uses a passive posture that signals they want to avoid hearing "no." Salespeople are generally nice people, so prospects don't want to hurt their feelings. Instead, buyers send subtle cues that, if recognized, provide clues about the root issue. Brian Tracy brilliantly articulated this point almost twenty years ago in his bestselling book *The Psychology of Selling*. He suggested that underperforming salespeople operate with subtle indirectness as a defense against the fear of rejection. But it's best to posture your communication more assertively in order to foster a more open, direct dialogue. Self-awareness is the igniter for improvement, so pay attention to . . . yourself.

As we think about the role of recognition and the RPD model in sales, two questions arise:

1. What does the "D" or decision-making part of the model represent?
2. And how does it relate to the PC process?

Given the natural perceptions on selling, we typically view the buyer as the only decision maker in the sale. However, selling involves pivotal decisions by sellers that have a strong influence on the sale. While some of these decisions are made after the interaction, many also happen in real time during conversation. In the next chapter, we will highlight several case stories to show how recognition and intuitive decision making is applied in real-world selling situations.

Situation Awareness

In 2009, pilot Captain Chesley B. Sullenberger, aka "Sully," encountered an engine failure when birds flew into his plane's engines shortly after takeoff. The Hudson River emergency plane landing of US Airways Flight 1549 is a textbook example of *situation expertise*. As Sully assessed the plane's predicament, he made a series of quick decisions based on intuitive skills acquired from his training and experiences. Sully was regarded as an expert in his field, having been specially trained in safety and emergency situations. But with all the years of training and experience, he had never landed an airbus in the middle of a river before January 15, 2009. His performance, however, was nothing short of superb. Have you heard the audio of the flight deck on flight 1549? The calmness in the captain's voice is hard to believe. His voice is steady, but you can feel his extreme sense of focus and decisiveness. That day, for the one hundred fifty-four passengers and crew on board, Captain Sully went from expert to hero.

The "Miracle on the Hudson" is a heroic example of ***situation awareness*** and decision making in a high-stakes setting. Moreover, it shows that situation expertise comes not through the rehearsal of specific situations, but rather the routine preparation for situations in general.

When experts face pivotal situations, their awareness is primed to respond timely and accurately. As such, the expert functions with a heightened sense of alert, expecting certain cues based on the scenario. Properly detecting these cues is important to improving intuitive skill. As you discovered from the Miracle on the Hudson story, preparation plays a key role in situational performance.

So with that said, what is the role of situation awareness in selling? While it is not life threatening to mishandle a sales objection, knowing how to adjust to situations is critical to success. In this segment, we will continue to explore the recognition in the context of common selling situations. Finally, you will have the opportunity to identify your own sales situations by completing the "Situation-Primed Insight Tool," located in Chapter 2.

Now, let's take a look at some of the most common selling situations and how to excel in them and optimize your odds for success. Most salespeople have targeted prospects who use a competitor's product or service. Competitive-selling scenarios may involve several factors such as:

- The timing of the engagement (Does it fit the prospect's timeline for change?)
- The nature of the competitor/customer relationship (Are they loyal? If so, how loyal are they?)
- The prospect's perceived capabilities of the competitor (Superior to yours? Neutral or inferior to yours?)

These types of factors make up the unique conditions of each situation. Another example might involve selling large-ticket items such as an enterprise computer system to Fortune 500 companies. In these cases, the prospect's internal silo effects and politics can often come into play. For instance, a proposed network computer system is often used in different ways by multiple departments. Many times, department silos create strained internal relationships that could lead to infighting, power struggles, or other problem behaviors. The sales rep or team will need to address these issues; otherwise, they could end up stuck with a time-draining, futile experience.

As we have discussed, it is not necessary to try and identify every possible situation you might face, but rather make sure that you master the most likely ones in your industry. The following list includes several of the most common **B2B** (*business-to-business*) selling situations:

- The prospect's objections and hesitations (fears and concerns)
- The prospect's product or service needs (implicitly expressed)
- The prospect's authority level (executive, mid-level, lower-level)

- The prospect's group and individual dynamics (one-on-one, one sales rep to two prospects, one sales rep to a group, one team to another team, etc.)
- The prospect's buying readiness and needs recognition
- The prospect's industry and business conditions
- The prospect's internal politics and silo dynamics
- Let us now look at each of these situations and how to recognize and address them effectively.

Explicit and Implicit Objections (Fears and Concerns)

For decades, salespeople have struggled to find ways to uncover and effectively handle a prospect's objections. Traditional sales training offers many techniques for overcoming objections that can add value to the seller's skill of handling them. However, it is important not to rely solely on techniques to deal with objections. There are two distinct types of objections: *explicit and implicit*. To effectively control objections, we first must define both types:

Explicit Objection—This is any type of prospect concern expressed *directly* as an obstacle or conditional issue that delays or stops the buying process.

Implicit Objection—This is any type of prospect concern expressed *indirectly* or that is masked as a different concern that delays or stops the buying process.

Novices tend to see more implicit objections because they lack connecting skills needed to foster more open and direct communication. On the other hand, skilled sellers and experts tend to see more explicit objections that are stated with more clarity and purpose. Since these types of concerns are discussed more openly, they are more likely to be resolved. To be clear, both experts and novices will experience explicit and implicit objections. But by and large, superior PC skills will invoke more explicit messages from prospects. For example, a prospect may introduce an explicit concern over not having funds budgeted for the proposed product. But suddenly an idea is brought up (by either party) that offers a way to move the sale forward.

With traditional sales training, objections are often reduced to mere requests for more information. This supports the notion that the salesperson was not clear enough in her presentation. The problem with this viewpoint is that it assumes the prospect does not have a valid concern. The salesperson may feel the need to go over the presentation again—in other words, she continues to talk instead of listen. Modern sales training models suggest a more shared, open approach to resolving objections. While this method is better than the old way, in many cases, the prospect may not have the answers to resolve the matter. In addition, more of today's buyers are addressing internal issues on their own without the help of salespeople. Hence, they may be headed toward a different solution that doesn't involve your product. Today's buyers access more sales material via the Internet and often use advanced purchasing teams to assess their needs. These trends helped to create the conditions for *insight selling* throughout the sales industry.

The shared approach to dealing with buying obstacles is good but has problems as well. For one, prospects often head down the wrong path because they lack the knowledge of better options. In addition, buyers tend to base the sale on *price* instead of focusing on *costs*. This can lead to purchasing errors that fail to meet the buyer's functional and financial return goals. Thus, it's critical that salespeople lead and not blindly follow the buyer's beliefs. They must guide the discussion and engage the prospect in the process.

As an example, after confirming an objection, a tech salesperson might say, "So, Jane, you mentioned that you don't think moving forward with the new software should happen until after your new CRM (customer relationship management) system is implemented. I do understand that concern, however, as you know, the ROI that you would give up by waiting another year would be substantial. Can you think of a way to find a balance between the CRM issue and making sure you get full advantage of the ROI from the new system?" The prospect may shrug their shoulders, and you could hear comments such as, "I have no idea" or "I'm not sure what we can do." Worse, the prospect may just suggest that you stop the sales process until a later time. While this may be the only alternative, a better approach may be to explore other options first. You might want to brainstorm ideas with the prospect before putting the options on the table to discuss them. It should be noted that most objections are triggered by salespeople who miss or ignore objection cues. As a result, the seller often assumes the sale is moving forward only to be *surprised* when the objection is raised during the close.

Handling objections is an integral part of selling. But the goal is to minimize them from stalling or threatening the sale. This can be achieved by (1) avoiding triggering implicit objections, and (2) encouraging explicit objections to surface earlier in the sale. Expert sellers use connecting skills that foster a more open, direct dialogue interaction. Within this context, prospects are more likely to express concerns as they arise. In section two, we will dive deeper into PC expertise and how it can be used to deal with customer concerns. But first, we will look at the objection-handling method and how to apply it effectively.

We have talked about avoiding the triggers that cause objections, but what exactly should you do once an objection is raised? This is the sixty-four-million-dollar question. Most of the sound objection-handling techniques taught in sales training include steps similar to these:

- Acknowledge the objection (so that the buyer knows he or she has been heard)
- Question the objection (to try to pinpoint the true concern)
- Answer the objection (problem solve and work together)

- Check that the resolution is suitable for the customer (make sure your answer was accepted by the buyer)

During my sales training classes, I often use humor to refer to these steps as "AQAC" (which sounds like the popular TV commercials for the company "Aflac"). Models like these can be useful in guiding your dialogue path, but keep in mind, they are not *the answer* for the objection. "AQAC" can therefore be used as a tool to express how you connect with the buyer and offer potential decisions to handle their objection.

Resolving objections involves three critical communication skills. First: Create an open and direct communication environment. Second: You must strive to detect objections early in the sales process. Third: You want to use effective questions to resolve concerns and advance the sale. Performing all three of these actions takes focused practice until they can be executed consistently well.

Often in sales training, objection-handling skills are taught in an impractical way. When was the last time you had a customer giving an objection by saying, "Hey, I'm getting ready to throw you an objection. I think your price is too high," or "I'm concerned about the risk of making this decision"? These types of objections used in a training context are oversimplified and ineffective. In reality, many objections tend to be much more implicit. Thus, implicit detection and intuitive skills are needed along with the right mindset to encourage more directness. A confident, trusting presence focused on the customer is the proactive way to stop objections from coming up at all.

In some cases, buyers may have obstacles that cannot be explained away or overcome through other means. These are known as ***conditions***. A condition might be a sudden policy change where a buyer can no longer make certain financial decisions. An example of this occurred during the height of the great recession—many businesses stopped authorizing long-term contracts. When banks tightened down on credit, businesses responded by avoiding new purchases in order to preserve capital. A condition does not always mean there is no chance to do business, but the sale will have to be made within the condition rules or at a later date. It is best for all involved to learn of these barriers before valuable time and effort is lost. *Intuitive skill* involves not only embracing early hesitations and objections but also expecting them. Expert sellers intently observe the prospect's message patterns when objections are raised. As we discussed, these patterns are cognitively matched to similar experiences (*recognition*).

In addition, the sales situation provides clues that allow you to predict the type of objection likely to come up. A good friend of mine and expert seller, Jason, is a sales rep who sells 401(k) plans. His expertise in his field of twenty years allows him to notice common situations for objections. Jason is able to access this knowledge when he encounters similar situations. For instance, he shared with me that he knows that smaller prospects that use a certain benefit provider are more likely to raise certain concerns. He cites the reason as a functional difference between the existing plan and his 401(k) offerings. As a result, he's mentally prepared for these concerns beforehand and handles them calmly and effectively when they arise.

Situation expertise relates to gauging the impact of an obstacle and making the right decision to handle it. Some salespeople ignore objections, apparently hoping the concern will go away on its own. While this could happen in rare cases, the reality is the sale often ends up stalling when a concern is not addressed. *Surprise objections* can cause the seller to become frustrated and send negative messages back to the customer. Buyers may notice this frustration through the seller's body language, tone, and increased *communication apprehension* (**CA**). By anticipating objections and viewing them as genuine prospect concerns, you remove the surprise factor. The fewer surprises you have, the more likely your sales message will be received.

When an objection is raised, use effective questions to pinpoint the underlying true issue and its cause. An "AQAC" type model can be helpful especially for implicit objections where more information is needed. The key to effective questioning is being genuine. You do not want to come across as too robotic, especially when asking probing questions as this could raise a red flag to the customer. To show genuineness, you must have the right mindset and goals. Remember, your attention should be process oriented and customer centered. To put it simply using a baseball analogy, don't think about hitting the homerun, instead focus on making the perfect swing.

When handling objections, your posture must be genuinely empathetic to the customer. Your interest in understanding the customer's concern must permeate the words and techniques you use. Even though we as salespeople would prefer not to have objections at all (not going to happen), it is essential to deal with them calmly and purposefully. My colleague and longtime good friend Mike Christie often uses the following analogy to show how to stay calm even when you might be a little nervous: Have you ever noticed a duck swimming in a pond? He looks to be as cool as a cucumber as he glides back and forth with what seems like little or no effort. But if you could see underneath the water surface, you'd find out that there's actually a lot of commotion and activity going on. The duck's feet are paddling frantically to move through the water. Expertise is about replicating the duck's approach, by mastering basic techniques such as AQAC (underwater paddling) behind the scenes so you are 100 percent engaged with the customer.

Product or Service Needs

The ability to match customer needs with your product or service is an essential skill of selling. Another common situation in sales involves the prospect's product or service needs. The goal is to understand the buyer's perception of their needs and adjust your sales message to match. In many selling industries, there are only a few different products or services that are sold. This simplifies matching customer needs to products and applications. However, many of today's organizations ask their sales force to sell more technically advanced products. This makes the task of noticing buying cues more challenging. Selling advanced products requires a broader understanding of business and product applications. Sellers who represent these offerings must develop large amounts of the right knowledge to connect offerings with prospect needs. Failure to recognize these critical cues and messages may result in leaving significant revenue on the table.

Strategies to Master Product Needs Situations

A notable skill commonly used by experts to grapple complex information is to break them down into "thin-slicing." The term was coined by Malcom Gladwell in his 2005 bestseller, *Blink*. Gladwell defines ***thin-slicing*** as a term used by psychologists to describe the human tendency to reach sophisticated conclusions based on very thin slices of experience. Expert sellers use thin-slicing to cut through complex product information and isolate the most critical factors. They're able to filter the few factors that matter the most. This thinking approach typifies the expert advantage for handling situations involving customer product needs.

A good example of thin-slicing in a product-needs situation can be found in the next example. Danette Ewald works as a logistics product specialist. In her role, she works large enterprise accounts to sell high-end transportation software products. Many sales reps struggle to learn these types of products due to the large amount of information surrounding them. But Danette leverages her years of customer experiences to thin-slice her product capabilities as follows:

- The Prospect's Order Management System Connectivity to Shipping System
- The Prospect's Current Carriers and Services Used
- The Prospect's Client Satisfaction (With Delivery) and Transportation Costs
- The Prospect's Need for Accessing of Post-Shipment Information

I've had the pleasure of joining Danette on several high-level sales calls. One of my key observations is that she does not consume her thoughts with the myriad of features and specs of the products she represents. Instead, her Spidey-sense guides her to the critical few areas that have the biggest impact on her customers' goals. She asks targeted questions within each of these four areas, which in effect narrowed the discussion to what mattered most while providing clarity for the customer to engage more openly. With each experience, patterns of recognition were matched to prior situations while new ones formed in tacit knowledge. Thin-slicing helped Danette become the sales expert she is today, and she continues to perform at the top of her profession.

Despite all of the sales awards and records she has broken, the thing that impressed me most about Danette is her short sales-cycle time. The logistics sale is one of the longer selling cycles in the software industry. Of the advanced product specialists in the company, most would only close one or two large deals each fiscal year. They simply took longer to understand the situation and sell the product in a timely way. But Danette routinely closed eight to ten high-revenue orders every year, making her one of the most consistent top performers in the logistics industry.

In many ways, thin-slicing goes against the conventional wisdom of diving deep into the details. It is the opposite of ***analysis paralysis*** syndrome. The notion of using less information to make better decisions is actually strongly supported by research. In *Blink*, Gladwell tells of a study in which emergency room surgeons performed better diagnosis of emergency situations of chest pain when they had less information to consider. The surgeons that were provided only four factors made profoundly more accurate diagnoses as compared to those who used more. But a vital key to thin-slicing is making sure that you are using the right factors. Thin-slicing skills can be cultivated through pattern recognition, experience, and well-designed training. In later chapters, we will discuss these development methods in more depth.

Chapter 2

SITUATION SELLING
LEVERAGING
CUSTOMER INSIGHTS

I n many B2B-selling situations, prospects often face acute obstacles or problems that inhibit the buying process. Typically, these problems have nothing to do with the salesperson or their company, but with a little creativity, the seller can provide insights that resolve the issue. A wholesaler might have trouble keeping track of returns or an insurance organization may have a problem tracking claims. Sellers learn of many of these issues during their talks with prospects. Most novice sellers move on unless the issue is directly linked to the sale. Skilled experts, on the other hand, take time to learn more, using their knowledge and experience to find helpful insights.

In this next case study, I introduce one of the finest selling experts I have ever met—Steve Hart. Steve's connecting skills helped him find a creative insight that resolved a huge problem for his customer. Steve and I worked together for four years at Pitney Bowes in the Sacramento area. As the government specialist, he handled our largest account: the State of California. In the early 1990s, the state was in the middle of a financial crisis whereby the budget did not get approved for several months. During this period, the state's largest agencies were unable to pay for many of their expenses, including postage. This meant not being able to send important mail using their Pitney Bowes postage machines. When Steve learned of the postage crisis, he jumped into action.

The Pitney Bowes Postage-By-Phone (PBP) business division provided postage refilling services for customers. The system was a prepaid postage service, meaning it required customers to mail a check before postage could be accessed. However, PBP would sometimes advance small postage amounts into a customer's account for emergency situations. This happened most often when customers forgot to mail in their postage checks.

Steve responded by devising a plan to allow the state postage advances, which were essentially loans worth several million dollars. He worked closely with state officials to make sure he knew what they needed. Steve's new insight essentially changed an existing prepaid postage method to a credit program. This allowed the agencies to use postage on credit for an extended period until their budget was passed. But this postage- on-credit concept was a huge paradigm shift from the way postage services were offered up to that point. Steve worked internally with PBP executives to develop the state's postage program before rolling it out.

The postage credit program was very successful. The state was able to continue mailing to their customers throughout the time period when they had no funds to pay for their services. As soon as the budget passed, they paid for the borrowed postage. Steve quickly became a popular figure among the state agencies, which, by the way, were delighted and thankful for what he had done. While on sales calls with Steve at several of these agencies, I saw them express their thanks firsthand. In fact, throughout his career until his retirement in 2011, the state remained a loyal customer. There are many similar stories of intuitive thinkers who drive creative new insights for customers. Think about your own experiences, and I bet you can find examples as well. The key to changing obstacles into insights is accessing knowledge and situations from your experiences.

Prospect's Appetite for Change

In 2002, Pitney Bowes acquired PSI, which was the nation's largest outsourced high-volume mailing service. This acquisition created Pitney Bowes Presort Services, a business unit that provides mail outsourcing to clients who produce high-volume mailings. (In exchange for outsourcing large mail volumes, the customer receives postage discounts and value-added delivery services.)

After a few years, the company wanted to expand the services to smaller volume customers. At the time, PSI had its own sales force that sold to high-volume customers. To penetrate the new low-volume market, the company decided to sell through its core sales channel, which consisted of over one thousand seven hundred reps. The offer was simple: Sales reps offered the service as a free add-on to mailing equipment sales they were already transacting. The best part was that they could earn commissions for placing the service, even though the customer paid nothing. In fact, customers received a small discount on their postage costs. (Presort service companies earn revenues via rebates from the US Postal Service, providing a value-added service to them.) Pitney Bowes was very excited about blowing out the numbers on the new service.

But when the results came back from the first quarter, they were disappointing. Management was perplexed as to why the product had not taken off. They tweaked a few things on the service by adding new features. When the year closed, the sales for the new program were still very anemic. But one sales rep in Boston, Adam Lewenberg, was having a field day selling the product. His placements were off the charts and no one else was even close. The marketing department decided to talk to Adam to discover his secrets to success. I recall listening to Adam at an event where he was speaking at a sales conference. He boiled his success down to this: "We sell mail services. In case you haven't noticed, mail is not exactly *sexy*. Because we sell this product that is free and isn't sexy, the biggest problem we have … is getting people to care."

I thought, *That's it!* Adam had analyzed the sales situation and recognized a pivotal issue that greatly impacted the sale: getting the customer to care enough to accept the "free" service. He offered several strategies on how to change the customer's view. The offer was simplified and presented in ways that were more compelling to the buyer. However, the silver bullet was not just his *response* to the situation, but also his *recognition* of it. The company learned from Adam's experiences and decided to re-launch the product, with much better success. Adam played such a major role in this turnaround that he was later assigned as the director to lead the product line. In his new role, the mail services revenue and new customers grew by fivefold over the next two years.

Understanding Customer Types

Within your customer and prospect segments lie common patterns for their appetite for change. These patterns can be leveraged (and not merely noticed) by adjusting your sales actions to fit the situation. In most sales markets, customers and prospects are broken down into segments. These segments could range from very broad ones like customers, noncustomers, and annual revenue, to more narrow categories such as existing customers using a certain type of product. For instance, during my years at McKesson Office Supply (wholesale), customer segments were grouped by annual revenue. In the office equipment industry, often criteria such as machine type and age are used. Although these profiles will vary, the key is to know how to angle your message based on each situation. A medical equipment salesperson would use a different message for a large hospital using high-tech million-dollar systems as opposed to a local clinic that uses twenty-year obsolete gear.

The Buying Process

Another common buying situation involves aligning the sales process with the buying process. You must remember that buying is not mutually exclusive to the selling. Novices tend to sell in a vacuum and do not adequately consider outside factors. As an example, a salesperson makes an appointment to present the product without knowing if the buyer is ready to evaluate options. Failure to recognize buying situations can lead to a loss of the buyer's interest. Buyers may feel they are being *sold* as opposed to *buying* when the seller's actions don't fit their goals.

This next story is a classic case of adjusting to the buyer's situation. While on a field ride-along with a sales rep, "Angie" adjusted to her customers just in time to save a great selling day. Angie had set up a well-prepared day. She scheduled meetings with existing customers, noncustomers, and prospects that used competitive products. After reviewing her sales planner, I was impressed and excited about the day ahead. Throughout the morning, however, as Angie made her presentations I noticed something odd. Each sales call sounded the same. The messaging she used for a customer with ten-year-old equipment was the same for that of a prospect using a competitor's equipment for just two years. As a result, Angie was unable to advance any of the prospects she spoke with that morning. At lunch, we had an opportunity to sit down and discuss how the morning went. I suggested to Angie that her sales message needed to adjust to fit each prospect's buying situation. To her credit, she agreed to make the necessary changes for the afternoon calls. The results for the rest of the day were much better. Angie closed a sale and advanced several other prospects further in her pipeline. She had customized her selling to each prospect's needs. For those that had older obsolete equipment, she talked about the potential of lost efficiency and increased maintenance costs. For competitive users with newer machines, she explored other areas that the competitor had not addressed. As a result, she was able to turn a bad day around while gaining new insights on the value of situation selling.

In short, a common mistake made in sales relates to noticing situations, but not making the adjustments. Different buyers in various situations will have varying degrees of interest in your sales offering. Interest level is driven largely by the buyer's appetite for change. Examples may include the perception of your product value and the degree of loyalty to you, your company, or another vendor. Thus, *situation selling* relates to adapting your sales strategy to match the buyer's interest level and value perception of your product.

(Table 2.1) compares several customer buying situations, buyer's value-need perceptions, and how a salesperson might adapt. This tool is designed to draw your attention to the buyer's perspective and to help you prepare your adaptive strategy. Sales scenarios will vary, but the basic principle—to align your selling process with the buyer's—remains.

Both buyers and sellers move through different stages of the buying and sales process. The sales process can become out of sync if not closely monitored. For example, in (Table 2.2) consider what would happen if the seller is at the *close* phase and the buyer is in the *recognition-of-needs* phase. Just because a sales step is executed does not mean the sale is ready to advance. The green light to move forward must always align with the buyer's readiness.

Heightened awareness and expertise can be expedited by recognizing these conditions in your work. Using the Situation-Primed Insight Tool (Table 2.3) as a guide, list the most common situations and insights you face in your sales market. You may also want to look for other areas where you may need improvements.

Table 2.1 Buyer Situations and Seller Adaptive Response

Typical Situation	Anticipated Obstacles or Opportunities	Situational Response by Salesperson
Objection or hesitation	• Buyer may need help overcoming an obstacle • Buyer may have underlying concerns • Buyer may not feel comfortable in selling engagement	• Refrain from "selling," and listen intently • Set aside counter-responses and self-interests • Seek the root cause objection and reasoning • Adjust sales approach
Advanced product or service needs	• Seller may need to qualify other people or departments • Profile high-potential opportunities and target • Seller accesses high level contacts	• Identify contacts for advanced products • Prospect to targeted lists • Start at higher level or transition to higher level early
Contact level	• Lower-level contacts will be more accessible, but you could get stuck at lower-level	• Start at higher level • Transition to higher level early in sales process • Adjust sales message to level of audience
Group individual dynamics	• Seller recognizes buyer's communication style • Seller adapts to buyer preferences • Seller recognizes group dynamics	• Notice style and preferences • Use connecting to build rapport • Adapt to style and preferences

Customer Appetite for Change	• Seller recognizes current product situation: customer, nonuser, competitor • Seller gauges buyer's interest level, timing, authority to act	Adjust sales approach to current disposition (high interest, low interest, compelling need to act, etc.)
Industry business conditions	• Seller recognizes industry situation (learn through research) • Seller learns buyer's company financial performance (learn through research)	• Prioritize contact plan (best opportunities first) • Adapt sales approach based on current conditions: for example, if high growth, reinvest in solution for sustained growth; for financial weakness, offer solution to reduce costs or enhance revenue
Internal silos or politics at play	• Fragmented communication across departments • Bureaucratic procedures • Infighting and envious relations	Proactively explore intercommunication effectiveness, and adjust accordingly
Sales process applicability	• Seller recognizes the value of the sale • Seller recognizes low or simple = transactional process • Seller matches selling situations with correct sales method • Seller recognizes buyer's preferences	• Predetermine the sales process based on product value or complexity • High quality for both sales processes • Adjust to buyer's buying process

Table 2.2 Comparison of the Sales Process to the Buying Process

Stages of the Selling Process	Stages of the Buying Process
1. Introduction or approach 2. Discovery or need development 3. Presentation 4. Close 5. Follow-up 6. Recycle (repeat #1)	1. Identification of potential problems 2. Recognition of needs 3. Evaluation of options 4. Negotiation of price or terms 5. Implementation of product or service 6. Recycle (repeat #1)

Table 2.3 Situation-Primed Insight Tool

Situation	Unique Elements of the Selling Situation	Potential Insights and Intuitive Reactions
Objections and Hesitations		
Product and Service Needs		
Contact Level		
Group Dynamics		
Prospect Internal Politics		
Customer Perceptions of Needs and Solutions		

Exercise

Think about your sales environment and fill in the above chart.

1. Describe the unique elements of your selling situation across the six common situations.

2. Reflect on previous sales experiences or knowledge from others' experiences and identify insights and potential reactions that were successful for each situation.

Contact Level (Executive, Mid-Level, and Lower-Level)

One of the most elusive situations in sales is accessing the right decision maker. In **B2C** (***business-to-customer***) retail, the key is to know whether the prospect is an *independent* or *co-buyer*. For example, a real estate agent selling to a married couple would want to engage both partners in the sales process. In the B2B context, salespeople can end up wasting precious time trying to sell to lower-level influencers rather than C-level executives. Based on their product's cost and complexity, salespeople work with people at various levels. In these scenarios, it's crucial to know when you need to move to the right level. It's also important to align your message to the priorities of the buyer once you recognize who you need to see. At times, these priorities may come into conflict at the different levels. For example, an operations person might push back on an automation concept for fear of reduction to her labor budget. Failure to access the right people can cost days and weeks of valuable selling time as well as lost sales.

I recently had a client who is the vice president of sales for a company in the print business equipment sector tell me that her sales force is "talking to the wrong people" about their solutions. She stated that most of her sales staff calls on shop managers of print shops instead of executives. An attempt to train up the team on how to reach executives proved to be unsuccessful. She estimated the problem was costing her organization about thirty million dollars in lost business! I was asked to survey the sales force to see what they thought. When asked why they were not accessing the executive level, the following responses by the sales force were given (common themes):

- Most of the time I do get to the right person or level.
- The decision makers are usually not in my territory (city or state).
- The executives tell me to go back to the shop manager.

- The shop managers will not allow us to go over their head.
- I do not know how to get to the top executives or what to say to them.

The following conclusions are based on the sales rep's collective responses:

1. The sales force did not see the issue as a major problem.
2. The sales force generally was content on talking to anyone who would listen and, as a result, did not put forth much effort into locating decision makers.
3. Management did not clearly convey the reasons they should engage with top executives.

Unfortunately, these types of responses tend to be consistent with many sales forces.

A key first step to improving your sales contact level is to decide that it is important and needed. Each sales organization may be different, but in general, access to higher levels is a key requirement for selling advanced products and services. Beyond the challenge of reaching the executive suite, sellers also are interested in selling to key sponsors. These are mid-level managers who drive new innovations within larger companies. Moreover, many sales industries require that sellers engage with multiple levels of contacts. In such cases, the seller must be able to navigate through different layers while adapting his sales message for each buyer.

Another inherent problem is the tendency for sellers to present the same message regardless of the level of contact. Novices tend to make this mistake because they are focused on what to say versus connecting to the buyer's message. Accessing the right level is only half the battle. Sellers must be able to adjust the sales message to connect to the level they are selling to. For instance, a COO is more likely to want to talk about the overall impact on operations versus how to use your product. A mid-level procurement manager is more focused on the product price and contract terms versus its benefits.

Sales professionals who want to improve in executive selling should consider a skills training workshop. The training must be targeted to fill the gaps in skills that are needed to improve performance. In general, top sellers use a simple three-step approach to access C-level executives:

1. *write* (letter, email, or fax),
2. *call* for appointment (after document is received), and
3. *meet* with the decision maker.

The *write-call-meet* approach has a proven track record of success in executive selling situations. Examples include the major account reps at Neopost USA, who use the strategy to penetrate high potential accounts. One of the hallmarks of the write-call-meet method is the *Access!* letter. This letter is aimed to garner the attention of C-level executives and decision makers because of its creative aspects and high-level tone. Neopost senior vice president Jay Singer, who created the letter as part of his Access! system, licensed its use to Neopost with positive results. Access! letters can be mailed or emailed, but a key to their success revolves around how they are addressed.

The idea is to find the highest level executive you want to engage and send her or him the letter. However, here's where it gets interesting: In addition to sending the letter to the key executive, original letters are also sent to other staff as well. Thus, the next step is to add several of the targeted executive's subordinates to the addressee list. Ideally, you want to identify two to three direct reports. The goal of sending original copies to the executive's staff is to create a sort of internal competition. This is known as **combustion**. Here's how it works: The letters arrive to each staff member, and they see the names of others who received the letter. Of course, no one wants to be left out of the loop, so combustion creates the internal conditions for action to take place. What often happens is the top executive will ask one of the staff to take the lead on the next steps.

Combustion can also be achieved using a vertical approach— that is, sending the letter to the executive's subordinate and their subordinates. Another way to generate combustion is by leveraging external competitive organizations. For example, if you were contacting an executive in the insurance industry, your Access! letter might indicate that you are planning to meet with other rival insurance companies (by name).

The Access! letter is a brilliant tool that I have personally seen work wonders. Figure 2.1 is a sample of an actual successful Access! letter used for the insurance vertical.

Figure 2.1 Sample of Actual Successful *Access* Letter

March 31, 20XX

Ms. Jane Doe

XXXXX XXXX Life Insurance

Address

City, ST. ZIP

Ms. Doe,

(1) I am writing this letter to you, John Smith and Joe Anderson (2) to determine who would be the most appropriate person to schedule a short meeting with in April when (3) I plan to speak with other senior executives of the country's most-respected Life Insurance firms.

(4) Specifically, my organization works with marketing executives in the insurance industry to:

- Increase customer retention and cross selling of products through optimized customer communications
- Create an effective e-delivery platform that has optimal opt-in rates and also generates effective digital marketing opportunities
- Ensure data quality to reduce document distribution costs associated with business critical customer communications

I understand through my research of your company that customer retention, customer expansion, and data quality are important to your future.

In analyzing your financial picture we believe we can have a $750,000 impact on your bottom line.

(5) We currently work with ABC Insurance, XYZ Insurance and we are confident that we can have a positive impact on your organization.

Next month, I plan on meeting with ABC Life and XYZ Life Insurance Co., and I will be following up the week of April 7th to see if you have an interest in meeting with me.

Thank you for your consideration, and I look forward to discussing this important opportunity with you soon.

Best Regards,
Neopost Sales Rep Name
Customer Communications Specialist
Neopost USA
Cell: XXX-XXX-XXXX
j.doe@neopost.com

Creating the Access! Letter (Formatting)

You begin by writing the Access! letter as shown in the sample in figure 2.1. As you can see from the sample, the letter uses business language designed to resonate with executives. Notice that the subordinates are named in the letter. In terms of how to mail, many sellers use different carriers such as FedEx, UPS, or the US Mail. The letter tends to get a much better response if it's mailed in a larger *flat-size* envelope (not folded). The following key explains the elements of the Access! Letter:

1. Purpose—Explains the objective and or purpose of sending the letter
2. Internal Combustion—Urgency created by including additional players within the executive's organization
3. External Combustion—Urgency created by referencing competitors of the executive
4. Insights, Benefits, and Pain Points to be addressed

Once the letter is received, it's time to secure the appointment. Remember, you are contacting a high-level executive so it may take several attempts to connect by phone. If the decision maker has a support person or assistant, try and make them an ally. He or she can often help you connect with the decision maker and navigate through their company's network.

A noted best practice for gaining higher-level access is to use an email calendar invite. Most email providers now offer this tool. However, you will need the recipients' email addresses to use it. To use the email invite, you should provide a conference call dial-in number for the group; but the preferred method is to try to connect directly with the top executive first before offering a group call. This gives you the chance to learn more about his goals without the staff being present.

Before making the call, make sure you are fully prepared. First, be sure to have several proof sources that you can quickly reference. Executives often will challenge you on whether you can deliver on the claims asserted in your letter. Second, write out the main talking points so you stay focused on your objective. This brings me to the final point of the phone call: ***the objective***.

The goal of the call is simply to invite the executive to a face-to-face meeting. If your industry requires air travel for meetings, you may want to suggest a phone meeting or video conference. You want to stay focused on the goal of securing the appointment. This is where sellers often make the mistake of trying to sell too early. Avoid this trap by politely, but confidently, inviting the executive to an appointment to explore the matter further. Before hanging up, tell him that you will be sending over an agenda for the upcoming meeting. This agenda should include all players on both sides who will participate. It also outlines the topics you plan to talk about with time allocations. Setting a time schedule and agenda is crucial because it shows that you are well organized and considerate of the executive's time. Senior managers do not want to waste time with salespeople who ramble through their presentation without purpose. See a sample agenda template in the appendix section of this book.

The initial meeting with the executive is often where sales are lost and won. It represents the first impression of who you are and the potential value you can offer. Thus, your goal is to present yourself as a skilled business-problem solver. The information contained in the rest of this book will help you be successful with executives. In addition, the ensuing chart (Table 2.4) lists objectives and actions for the initial executive meetings.

Group Dynamics in the Selling Environment

In 2000, my solution sales team at Pitney Bowes consisted of a senior sales executive, two technical product specialists, a sales manager, and me. We formed the team a year earlier to focus on selling to our high-potential revenue accounts and prospects. When a large

Table 2.4 Objectives and Actions for the Initial Executive Meeting

OBJECTIVES	ACTIONS
Understand decision maker (DM) goals	Establish business rapport Ask questions
Educate—Inform DM of your value	Present capabilities (Brief)
Understand DM priorities	Ask explicit priority questions
Qualify opportunity (Ready, willing, able)	(After business rapport is established) Ask qualifying questions
Gain Commitment to Advance	Lay out Next Steps and Timelines

sales opportunity with a manufacturer in Los Angeles arose, the team engaged. We set up a meeting at the customer's site with the general manager and his operations team. The presentation began as planned and seemed to be going well. The sales rep reviewed the customer's needs and our capabilities. When the IT director raised a technical question, one of our tech specialists responded and discussed the issue. The dialogue expanded until it morphed into a full-blown technical conversation. Before I knew it, more than an hour had passed as they discussed the topic. That's when the general manager (GM) announced that he had to leave for another meeting, but he asked if we would continue without him. The meeting ended up turning into a disaster. Needless to say, we never saw the GM again, nor did we earn their business.

As a result, I called my team together to discuss what had happened and how we could improve our team-selling process. Several improvements emerged from our work as follows:

1. We installed presales meetings whereby we allocated procedural rules and established specific roles for each team member.

2. We developed a detailed agenda for each meeting that included presenters, topics, and allocated times (the birth of the agenda document).

3. We developed a code alert system that allowed us to communicate with each other during selling interactions without the customer being aware. For instance, a team member could alert a speaking team member to engage the customer more if it was perceived that the customer was getting bored or disinterested. To do this, the team member might cough for attention then grab his ear (indicating the need to listen). Our team-selling continued to improve for years until it was more than just a set of rules; it had actually evolved into part of our selling proposition.

A few months later, the team found itself in a similar meeting with a large biotech laboratory company. Although the players were similar, our sales process was much improved. Prior to our presentation meeting with this customer, the sales rep who handled the account—Regina Johnson—and our internal sales team met to discuss the upcoming meeting. We went through the different parts of the presentation, including anticipated questions. Our enhanced team-selling process clarified the roles of each member of the team. We learned that technical discussions, if left unmanaged, could derail our presentation. In response, our team addressed this issue by setting up technical presales meetings (usually via conference call).

Regina ended up closing a $1.2 million sale, one of the largest in the company that year and nearly twice her annual quota. Moreover, the team had learned valuable lessons on team selling to a group. After a successful implementation, I spoke with (NAME) the COO who had authorized our sales order, asking him why he decided to entrust his business with us. I expected to hear him mention the financial and operational savings to his bottom line. Instead, he told me that our sales process made the difference in his decision. He cited our procedures as standing out from the other competitors. Regina's success story was written in the company's sales newsletter. Here is a quote from Jim, the VP of Operations (key decision maker): "The Pitney Bowes sales team used a process-oriented sales approach, which gave us the confidence that they were capable to deliver the solution we needed. Other vendors talked a good game but their process did not back it up."

I thought, *Wow, so our sales process, in and of itself, added value to our proposition.* This was an eye-opening lesson on selling to a group dynamic that I've tried to share with others ever since.

Internal Politics and Silos

Another common challenge of selling to enterprise groups is dealing with politics and silo mentalities. *Silos* relate to organizations where some people or departments do not want to share knowledge and information. Customer internal politics, infighting, or silos can thwart any sales opportunity if not properly managed. In my sales director role at Pitney Bowes Presort Services (PBPS), we faced a silo situation that stalled a sale for over a year. Recall that PBPS provides mail outsourcing to clients who produce high-volume mailings. Erick Norman, who was the account manager out of Northern California, had been working with a financial services customer for over a year. At the time, we were handling a small portion of their mail, but the largest volumes were in the hands of a competitor. Erick, one of our top sales reps, was doing everything he could to earn more of the customer's business; but whenever he met with the buyers and asked questions regarding the other mail volumes, he got the cold shoulder. The operations manager would usually say, "It's out of my hands." One day, while speaking to Erick on the phone, we reviewed target prospects for my upcoming visit. I asked about the financial services account and what we could do to advance the sale. Erick decided to set up an appointment for us to visit.

A week later, we met the operations manager for lunch. There, Erick asked questions about their concerns. This time, however, his questions were more penetrating and probing. Erick's tone and message came across as needing to know the concern in order to find out how he could help. The operations manager finally decided to open up and explain. She lowered her voice and proceeded to describe an internal battle that had been raging between two departments for some time. One very influential department head, whom I will call "John," liked the competitor and wanted to keep them, while the other department wanted to work with us.

Armed with this feedback, Erick reached out to John and learned about his particular views and interests within the company's operations. After evaluating the current proposal that was on the table, Erick made specific changes to it based on John's feedback. The proposal was resubmitted to the key department heads, including John, who previously was not provided his own copy. As one of our top producers, Erick was a very charismatic person. He used his intuitive presence to reverse the stalled account and uproot the obstacle. Within a short time, he earned a new sales order that included the remaining volumes of mail. I believe what made the difference in Erick's last sales call was his intuitive posture, which led to the ops manager exposing the issue. By adapting his sales message to the situation, Erick broke through the gridlock and helped his customer achieve its business goals.

Chapter 3

THE ANATOMY OF EXPERT SALES PERFORMANCE

Experts, Journeymen, and Novices

B efore we can go any further in our journey to expertise, we must first understand the structure of expert sales performance by addressing several key questions:

1. Who can be deemed an expert and what standard should be used?
2. What are the main components and skills that drive expert sales performance?
3. How do experts become experts?

This chapter also serves as a glossary of sorts, where we define several key terms and concepts that are used throughout the book. The goal is to reduce doubt by level-setting key terms to maximize clarity. This understanding helps to give you a solid foundation to gain knowledge from *Expert Selling*.

The academic definition standard for *expert* suggests a *world-class* level performer. However, researchers on expertise in natural settings (e.g., business) tend to rely on the more practical definition of *superior performer*. In this context, an expert performer is someone who consistently performs better than other performers. A *journeyman* is characterized by a solid track record of experience with adequate skills and performance. Journeymen are your typical *advanced performers* who aspire to move to the expert level. *Novice* sellers have limited or no experience, basic skills, or a history of subpar sales results.

I am often asked, "Are the top producers always the experts?" Perhaps the top producer has the best territory, or maybe he is assigned the highest revenue accounts. Because of these and other factors, be careful not to equate results alone to expert performance. However, as you will discover later in this chapter, there's a causal link between skill, performance, and results. Expertise is marked by consistent and overall performance excellence.

The use of the term *expert* tends to vary from industry to industry. Therefore, it is important to overlay your particular industry guidelines with the definitions just described. That being said, experts always know who they are. Award-winning blogger and entrepreneur Corbett Barr said it best: "You don't have to be the world's greatest expert. It's about being *expert enough* to accomplish your goals."

Our working definition of *performance* is to *consistently execute a task well*. The premise of this book's focus is *individual* performance as opposed to *organizational* performance. Organizational performance includes internal environment factors that influence outcomes such as compensation systems, infrastructure, culture, and management. External factors, including the economy and competition, also play a role in organizational performance. Most salespeople work as part of a team that is connected to a company structure. Therefore, it's important to understand how sales reps drive organizational performance, and likewise, how the organization's work environment affects sales rep production.

We have learned now that personal and organizational performance affects the other, but how do they impact *sales performance*? To answer this question, we first must define sales performance. We can think of it as a structure of three cylinders—capability, execution, and results—as indicated in Figure 3.1.

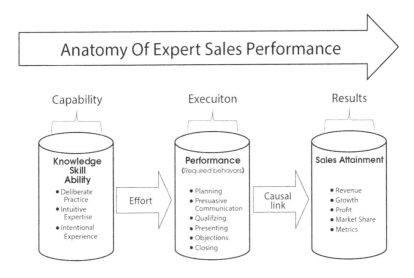

Figure 3.1 The Anatomy of Expert Sales Performance

Capability: (Tacit) Knowledge, Skills, and Actions

The totality of a salesperson's *knowledge, skills, and actions* (KSA) plus their effort determines capability. Knowledge is what you know, skill is how you perform, and actions equate to applying what you know to your work. The "A" in KSA also represents *ability*, which is marked by innate potential. KSAs cover a variety of sales-specific disciplines relative to job duties. To achieve a standard of success, many sales careers and roles require certain KSAs and experience. For example, a medical equipment sales position that markets high-end MRI machines might seek a more technically inclined salesperson. Therefore, people who are entering sales for the first time should target sales organizations with products that best suit their skillset. A formal skill assessment can be used to shed light on your KSA strengths and areas to improve. They can also help you decide on the right sales industry or product offering that's right for you.

Whether it's sales or another business segment, employees must acquire a basic KSA level to competently perform their jobs. Most of these skills are acquired from company-sponsored training activities; however, once basic competency has been achieved, sellers grow skills mostly through experience. Hence, expert sales performance is marked by *tacit knowledge* and *situation awareness*, built through *implicit learning*. Implicit skills are largely subconscious and the performer is often unaware of their presence or unable to express them. Although these skills may be hard to pinpoint, their impact on performance is unmistakable.

Consider a football quarterback and his role in leading his team to the winning touchdown. There are distinct differences in the few great quarterbacks who seem to make the right decision when it matters most. Many NFL quarterbacks have good arms and other athletic skills in general. For the most part, they are skilled enough to play well in most games. They call the play, know where the pass is designed to go, read the defense, and execute the pass to the receiver. But for the NFL quarterback, the *window of expert advantage* can be found within *recognition skills* and *situation awareness*. Can he make the right pass decision at the end of the game when every play is critical? The elite players develop the skills that allow them to quickly recognize the defensive coverage before and after the snap. Finally, a top quarterback executes the pass with accuracy by completing it for the game-changing play or winning touchdown. And by the way, these decisions are made in less than three seconds while a two-hundred-seventy-pound linebacker bears down on him from his blindside.

Throughout these high-pressure conditions, the top quarterbacks deliver this type of expert performance. When the game is on the line, their performance separates even more from other players. Top quarterbacks such as Tom Brady (New England Patriots) or Aaron Rodgers (Green Bay Packers) are excellent examples of players who perform their best in the clutch moments of games. While most quarterbacks never make it to the Super Bowl, many of the top-tiered players have multiple championship appearances and wins.

People often relate tacit knowledge and situation awareness with natural talent or special gifts. To the contrary, research on expert performance reveals that a major difference in expert and typical performers is continual learning with progressive difficulty. Psychologists and learning experts describe the three stages of learning a new skill as (1) cognitive, (2) associative, and (3) autonomous. Let's look at these stages in the context of learning to drive a car. The cognitive stage is expressed by forming a picture of the overall concept of driving (instruction, observation, and feedback). For instance, a novice driver reads the steps of driving in the driver handbook and observes a parent driving. The associative stage is represented by practicing the skills of driving (practice, refinement, and recognition of errors). Example: The novice driver practices driving with a parent or driving instructor and receives coaching. In the autonomous stage, the learner performs the skill automatically and with minimal effort (skill automaticity, self-correct errors, ability to focus attention on other cues within the environment).

Example: A driver easily drives to her destination, while engaged in a conversation and drinking a bottle of water.

Dr. K. Anders Ericsson, the research expert on expertise who was mentioned earlier in this book, asserts that experts continue to engage in the *cognitive* and *associative* stages of learning by developing increasingly complex representations to attain higher levels of controls over their performance. Lesser-skilled performers tend to remain in the *autonomous* stage (the third stage of learning), once the skill becomes easy to perform. Experts, however, continue to grow knowledge and skill through unique learning tasks, thereby increasing performance.

Deliberate Practice: How Experts Become Experts

Everyone knows that practice is important to improving skills; who hasn't heard the old adage "practice makes perfect"? Practice in the most basic sense achieves the goal of transferring a skill for permanent use. But for expert performance, practice must have a stronger element of quality and intention. For example, a novice golfer might practice his game by going out and playing a round of golf. But the expert golfer, one of the greatest golfers in the world, practices much differently. He or she might take an entire day just working on one particular shot, such as a sand bunker chip shot. The expert hits the same shot over and over until muscle memory and execution is consistent. To add difficulty, they may change the ball's lie or the angle of the shot in order to account for varying factors that could occur during an actual performance. Last, the expert's practice is goal specific. Rather than just hit balls for a certain amount of time, he may hit hundreds of shots until one hundred of them are successful. Thus, we improve upon the old adage to say, "Practice makes permanent; deliberate practice makes perfect."

The primary ingredient of expert performance can be can be traced to *deliberate practice,* a unique training method specifically designed to improve performance. Three tenets of deliberate practice include repetition, immediate feedback, and progressive difficulty. Usually directed by a skilled coach, it is most often applied in performance settings involving large amounts of practice such as sports and music. Hence, much of the research on deliberate practice has been focused on world-class athletes and top musicians, but in recent years it has also been applied in natural settings including business.

The obvious difference between athletes and musicians versus salespeople is the availability of practice time. Most professional sellers work eight or more hours a day, leaving little time for sharpening skills. That said, you should seek to carve out time for practice wherever possible. Whether rehearsing your presentation or polishing demo skills, practice helps to drive skill improvement. Even with limited time constraints, deliberate practice can help speed up skill improvement. In today's fast-paced world, there are many distractions that manage to occupy our minds. But the right practice is worth the time because it produces a positive impact on performance.

Deliberate practice research has shown it to be a scalable activity based on frequency and duration. For instance, world-class athletes engage in the activity three to four hours a day, six days a week, and for ten years or more. However, many performers who fall into lower tiers still benefit from lesser amounts of deliberate practice.

Most salespeople want to improve performance to a level that allows them to achieve their goals and personal growth. They are less concerned with achieving world-class level in selling. But the better news is knowing that your KSA development can take you as far as you want to go.

Since professionals don't have much time for extended practice, there's been an effort to find other ways to learn while working. Experts Dr. Peter Fadde and Dr. Gary Klein define **deliberate performance** as an effort to increase domain expertise while engaged in routine work activity. If you replace the word *domain* with *sales*, you have the definition of Performance-Based Learning® (PBL). PBL sales activities will be covered in more depth in section three. For now, we will focus on the framework of deliberate practice and performance, which are the key drivers to systematic improvement of selling KSAs. Figures 3.2 and 3.3 depict the key elements of deliberate practice and deliberate performance, respectively.

Figure 3.2 Key Elements of Deliberate Practice

Figure 3.3 Key Elements of Deliberate Performance

Deliberate practice training coupled with PBL during routine work hastens connecting skills improvement. Now that we've examined the KSA components' selling capability, we turn our focus to *effort* and *execution*.

Effort: We Know a Lot More Than We Do

During the 2000s I worked with a very good salesperson who for the sake of her privacy I will call "Jane." In reviewing sales reports, I noticed Jane's sales production was down significantly. In prior years up until that point, she was very successful with Pitney Bowes. Although Jane was still able to do her job and achieve her sales quota, the volume of her sales revenue was down by 40 percent. I decided to set up a meeting with her to help identify and solve the problem. This meeting evolved into multiple meetings over several days. Even though I had a very good professional relationship with Jane, she became defensive when we discussed the potential reasons for her drop in performance. She blamed the CRM system and other departments and even pointed the finger at her sales manager for her shortfalls.

Eventually, Jane shared with me what was going on. It turned out that because of personal family reasons, she was unable to make more than one or two sales calls per week. To my surprise, I learned that this had been going on for over a year, matching her decline in performance. I reminded Jane that great skill with low activity will produce only modest results at best. Simply put, while excellent selling skills are essential to success, there is no substitute for the value of effort. Selling at a high level requires engagement in many activities. These can include making calls, learning from experiences, engaging customers and internal colleagues, and developing skills. The list goes on further. Professional selling is not easy by any stretch, but one essential factor of success is giving your best effort every day.

A notable contrast can be observed between salespeople who work hard and those who work but tend to waste valuable selling time. The sales culture is deadline driven. Therefore, sales reps who misuse time are less productive. For instance, in sales offices or retail stores, sellers often interact and socialize. But timewasters tend to continue these conversations for much too long. They work on paperwork for hours or strike up personal conversations that erode time that could otherwise be used to advance the sale. Many sellers now operate out of home offices. Yet time is wasted on phone calls or on other non-selling activities.

Let me premise my next statement with this: Top producers are not *always* the hardest workers. But by and large, the most consistent top producers tend to work very hard. Contrary to timewasters, productive reps are acutely aware of what we call **optimum selling time** (**OST**). In most B2B sales, OST is between eight a.m. to noon and one p.m. to four p.m. In the retail space, OST might apply to the weekend shift and evenings. The idea is to maximize OST for customer interactions. Unlike timewasters, productive sellers act as if they have an OST clock in their head—a fierce sense of urgency. They set personal rules on using their time wisely and can even get antsy if you hold them up for long. Simply put, they work hard and they work smart, and they never waste time.

In sum, top producers aren't top producers simply because of skill alone. They learn to leverage skill by applying it in more situations. Thus, expertise is formed not through mere experience but through *experiences*. Effort drives the selling activities, which become your experiences. This does not mean that more is always best, but it's important to do *enough* of the right activities every day. Thus, effort plays an essential role in the execution of expert sales performance.

Moving from Effort to Passion

Have you ever noticed that successful people seem to have very high levels of motivation? Are they born with this burning drive to get up early and work fourteen-hour days? While conclusive evidence is lacking, several theories have emerged that offer some explanation. Some believe that top achievers are driven by success, rewards, and recognition. Many psychologists point to innate talents or environmental factors such as family upbringing when describing what is known as ***achievement motivation***.

Frankly, I think Geoff Colvin nailed it in his book *Talent is Overrated: What Really Separates World-Class Performers from Everybody Else* when he said, "We simply don't know." But whether it comes through praise from parents and admirers or through the realization of success, passion and expert performance seem to feed off the other. My hypothesis is that passion is closely related to performance achievement. Outstanding performance fuels the desire to continue to excel to even higher heights.

Consider LeBron James, arguably the best basketball player in the NBA. By winning the NBA Championship back to back, he finally answered his critics who questioned whether he could win multiple championships. But as you will see from the upcoming excerpt from a LeBron interview, he remains focused on getting better. The following interview was done six days after winning his second NBA title:

"It's something that I want again. Because the time goes fast. We won it Thursday night, and we've already had the parade.… I want to be able to win another championship because it's the best feeling in the world. I want it…"

Success can be a vicious cycle, but the passionate drive to succeed is quite common in the world of top performers.

Everyone can relate to the idea of gradually building momentum of motivation through incremental successes. For example, recently my doctor told me that I needed to lose weight because my blood glucose levels had approached the pre-diabetes level. I was told that if I did not make changes in my habits, my health could be at risk. First of all, the mere mention of the word *diabetes* scared the daylights out of me. My doctor suggested that I lose twenty pounds in six months. I had always been a reasonably healthy person, so it was a bit of a shock to discover that I now *had* to change my diet and get more active. I decided to make changes to my eating habits and commit to running four times a week. I knew the diet would be the hardest thing because I'm a guy who likes his sweets, but after working out and changing my diet for just a couple of weeks, I weighed myself and saw that I had lost six pounds! This measurable result motivated me to do even better. I began to intensify my workouts and even started counting calories to meet my goal. After only a month, I lost ten pounds. I was excited and feeling better physically. In just over two months, I lost the entire twenty pounds. I decided to stop by my doctor's office and let him know that I had done it! My second round of blood tests showed that my glucose levels were back to within normal range.

In my case, stepping on the scale and seeing the pounds drop represented evidence of achievement. This in turn spurred me to continue and follow my commitment to living a healthier lifestyle. It was simple; a weight loss goal was set by my doctor, I noticed progress, my drive became stronger to achieve and exceed the goal. In many ways, passion and expert performance is remarkably like the chicken and the egg—you may not know which came first, but you certainly know that one comes from the other.

"No, *you* back off! I was here before you!"

Execution

So far, we have defined the key elements of KSAs and performance *capability*; now we will discuss *execution*, which relates to effective action. Execution is the act of applying the skills to the specific activities needed for success. In this context, we assume that the organizational factors are supportive and free of toxic inhibitors. All things being typical, excellent sales KSAs and great effort drive the desired actions.

How can salespeople execute more effectively? Although it will vary in different selling industries, execution boils down to consistently performing the basics well. Experts in many domains seem to have the ability to deliver the right performance at the right time.

Preparation plays a key role in performance capability. Whether it be practice for an expert musician or an executive in business planning, we know that experts prepare to perform at the highest levels.

Another important factor in execution involves *attentionality*, which relates to laser focus during performance. To understand attentionality, we first discuss the effects of the wrong attentions. Consider a basketball team that is trying to win every game by thinking about winning. As each game unfolds, players focus on scoring more points than the opponent, but their play suffers. When the star player thinks of making the game-winning shot, he misses it. Sports science and all good basketball coaches will tell you that this type of results-oriented mindset can be toxic to the players' play.

Great teams use attentionality to win. For example, they focus on making the right passes, getting more rebounds, and making their free throws. The team narrows its focus on its play, not the desired results. These performance principles are applied in natural settings as well. During an operation, the expert surgeon doesn't think of the patient's full recovery, she concentrates on removing the tumor and preparing for any potential adverse situations. As such, selling at a high level requires a heightened awareness of the selling-execution process rather than result outcomes. To put it simply, experts focus on the aspects within their control rather than the outcomes they cannot.

Last, superior performance is driven through *progressive improvement*. Selling experts identify the most critical parts of their skills, then create a plan to improve them. The performance process includes preparation, pinpointed focus, and progressive improvement carried out daily. This success routine fosters automaticity, but is occasionally disrupted with new learning to avoid arrested development (AD). In short, **_sales performance_** is made up of several interacting parts—**_KSAs_**, **_effort_**, and **_execution_** that drive performance results. These parts have a direct link to sales results, which we will cover next.

Causal Linkage to Results

As we've discussed, capability, effort, and execution are all within the span of control of the seller to execute and improve. Let's use the example of Cindy, a B2B sales rep in the software sector. Cindy can improve her KSAs through training, practice, experience, and observing other performers. Of course, she controls her own effort as well. She gets up each day, plans her work, and does what is necessary to produce results. While outside influences can affect her motivations, it's Cindy's personal choice to work hard and be her best every day.

But what about the results? Are we able to control the outcomes and results in the same manner as we can control our capability and efforts? The answers may vary depending on the circumstances. Perhaps golfers or Olympic swimmers have the ultimate control over their results compared to salespeople whose success in part depends on many other factors and players. But even golfers can hit the ideal shot or play the hole perfectly, only to have another player do it even better. In other words, golfers or swimmers may be able to control their own results to an extent, but the outcomes are still subject to outside factors.

Coaches understand that there are games in which the team may play well but still lose and conversely, there are games where the team may *not* play well and win. They know that the odds are stronger on the side of winning when the players focus on execution and playing their best.

Perhaps in sales this principle is even more meaningful and appropriate given the relative weight placed on results. Business executives, managers, and sales professionals often have their job security and income tied to their performance. I used to always greet my new-hire sales training classes with a big smile and say, "You decided to get into sales because there is no ceiling to your income, right?" All the heads would nod and big grins would appear. Then I'd say, "But guess what? There's also no floor!" As looks of shock replaced the smiles, I would inform them that our goal was to ensure that they stayed closer to the ceiling than the floor. My little icebreaker achieved its point of garnering the class's attention, but truth be told, it's a fact that earnings are the holy grail of selling.

Sales Results and Metrics: Evidencing Expertise

There are typically three result-based metrics that are paramount to any sales professional: *sales quota*, *sales revenue growth*, and *sales profit margins*. While these fall under the category of quantitative results, most organizations also measure qualitative metrics such as *conversion rates*, *customer satisfaction*, and *customer retention*, to name a few. Results reflect the end goal and the primary reason that sales forces exist. Companies are driven to make a profit. Achieving top-line revenue is the first step in attaining overall profit objectives. Of course, good companies must also manage expenses to optimize profits from their revenues. Growth metrics are used by many organizations to drive long-term success. No matter how much you sell in a given year, you get to try and repeat it the following year! In fact, many organizations now include growth elements within sales quotas. Results metrics are a reflection of sales performance outcomes. Understanding the elements that affect performance gives you knowledge to adjust your personal actions to impact results.

Performance Consistency:
There Are No Trophies Given Out at Halftime

OK, we now know that capability plus effort drives results. Therefore, expert capability plus high effort creates outstanding performance. The reason we can say this with confidence is that the common unit of business performance measurement is one year. Legendary basketball coach John Wooden said it best: "If you make the effort to do the best you can, regularly, the results will be about what they should." Certainly, no one can question Coach Wooden's results: ten national titles in twelve years, including seven in a row.

Although salespeople are measured monthly, or quarterly, the most important timeframe is the fiscal year. In most sales settings, the element of time acts as a great regulator. When a seller with good KSAs and effort executes for the year, his results tend to match his performance. By using a shorter time range, such as monthly or quarterly, more exceptions will occur. Put another way, in any given month, any capable seller can generate good results. On the flip side, a consistent performer may have an off month or two during the year; this happens to everyone. However, in sales, time has a funny way of autocorrecting the numbers. By year's end, more often than not, your results will line up to your performance.

Chapter 4

EXPERT ATTITUDE AND SELF-AWARENESS
"YOU ARE WHO YOU THINK YOU ARE"

Professional Integrity and Ethics

I n psychology, the idea of a positive self-concept is essential to people's experience of life. Likewise the self-concept of the salesperson must be strong and positive to perform at a high level. We see every day the value that salespeople bring to our overall economy. When consumers and businesses buy, capital is active, which creates momentum and confidence in the financial markets. However, somewhere in its past selling got a bad rap, and now some people prejudge sellers as being manipulative or deceptive. Perhaps it was the era of the fast-talking traveling salesman. They were known for blitzing towns and convincing unsuspecting buyers into purchasing goods that often did not work; and unfortunately, even today there are a few people who make unethical choices that can damage the credibility of a great profession. Such a situation is evident in the story to follow. While there may be a temptation to minimize the truth to get a sale, it is essential to be true to yourself by being honest and trustworthy.

While in my role as sales director at Pitney Bowes, a competitor recruited away several of our longtime employees. Months later, a sales employee for the same competitor contacted one of our senior managers seeking employment. As the process evolved, I had the chance to interview the salesperson, whom I will call "Mark." After interviewing him, I came away with serious concerns about his professional integrity and ethics. He did not seem to be a good fit for our culture, which had very high ethical standards. When asked questions about his sales approach, Mark's response suggested that he used bait-and-switch type tactics. The worst part for me was the fact that he seemed unaware that these were deceptive sales practices.

Despite these concerns, and for reasons that I cannot get into, Mark was hired by the company. The first thing I did was sit down with him and explain our standards of professionalism policies. I also went over the ethical standards and expectations for all employees. His response was neutral; he did not embrace what I had to say, but at the same time he agreed to follow the rules. Within a few weeks, problems began to surface regarding his interactions with other sales employees in our office. It was reported that Mark was engaging in deceptive phone discussions with prospects that could be heard from his office. When asked if he had misinformed a customer, he intimated that our company's approach to customers was "too nice to get results." As time passed, other employees grew very concerned and described his attitude as desperate to get any sale. We also continued to receive negative feedback on Mark's work. Moreover, his sales production was virtually nonexistent after nearly a year on the job. He was counseled on how to improve his sales activities but instead he continued using his old methods. Eventually, he separated from the company.

The bottom line is that Mark was unable or unwilling to change his behaviors to function in a professional, high-standards work culture. Instead, he continued to embrace his old behaviors, which failed miserably. I don't know his full background, but I do know that anyone who uses unethical practices eventually pays the price for their actions—the price of lost sales from distrusting prospects as well as jeopardizing their ability to earn a living in sales. Deception has no place in professional selling. Nothing is worth sacrificing your personal and professional integrity. No sale, large or small, is worth risking your credibility. Hopefully, Mark was able to learn from his mistakes, but it's these types of behaviors that often lead to increased sales resistance and create bad perceptions of salespeople. This leads to unnecessary sales resistance from buyers that makes it harder for honest, hardworking reps to do their jobs.

Human psychology plays a role in everything we do. The way we think drives our behaviors and performance. Our attitudes and moods affect how we approach our work and other aspects of our lives. Although the mind is a complex thing, you should not shy away from trying to know yourself better. Learning how you think and about your cognitive tendencies is an important prerequisite for developing expertise. Aspiring experts must learn the valuable skill of self-evaluation in order to advance their skills to the next level. This doesn't mean trying to analyze all of your thoughts and beliefs; it simply means being aware of your thinking enough to recognize when adjustments are needed. I like to say it this way: "You have to get your mind right to perform right." To be at your best when it's time to perform, you must first be the expert seller in your mind and in your heart. Thus, it is necessary to regularly assess your mindset openly and honestly. By opening yourself up to acknowledging the flaws and gaps in your skills, you create the best conditions for improvement. In sum, you first master yourself before you can master your craft. We now discuss the following mental inventory as part of your self-evaluation and improvement process. Ask yourself:

- Do I demonstrate strong personal and professional integrity and ethics?
- Am I able to control sales anxiety and relax when I need to?
- Do I exhibit self-confidence?
- Do I engage in continuous development and learning?
- Do I set and achieve performance goals?

As sales professionals, we must maintain the highest ethical and professional standards in all we do. I believe that our personal character is a reflection of our work and our personal values. To quote Shakespeare, "This above all: to thine own self be true." These words ring true in sales, as I believe that most sellers have good character and are decent, honest people. But we all must bear the responsibility of making sure that we are following the highest ethical standards in selling.

If you're serious about moving your performance to the next level, you must bring with you a high level of integrity and ethics. The expert seller functions with openness and honesty at all times. Let me be clear, you don't have to open up your price book to all your prospects just to be open, but you do need to provide full disclosure of any and all information that they should know. The most common mistake in this area is a sort of ***rolling disclosure***, which is the idea of withholding information until the last minute or until it is detected by the buyer. For example, a seller might delay informing a customer of an extended delivery date or backorder that could be seen as unfavorable by the buyer. But if the salesperson is silent about issues like backorders, the customer may assume a best-case scenario that is impossible to achieve.

Too many sales reps try to avoid disclosure discussions. And by the way, slipping a document or a website link to the customer with little or no explanation is not good enough. This is not selling with the highest level of integrity. The right thing to do is to promptly disclose important information to the customer and work with them to resolve any issues that may arise as a result.

Ask yourself, "How would I want a salesperson to treat me if I were the customer?" Unfortunately, I have seen really good salespeople destroy fifteen- or twenty-year careers because they decided to make a dumb choice. You must be trustworthy, reliable, and professional at *all* times. Your customers will appreciate and honor your integrity by entrusting you with more business. Moreover, by maintaining a high ethical standard, you avoid falling into the trap of trying to be *the* best at the expense of being *your* best.

Overcoming Communication Apprehension (Sales Anxiety)

Ji-Yoon was a relatively inexperienced sales rep who worked in my district sales office. Although she was new to B2B sales, she worked very hard to learn as much as she could and improve her skills. One day it was announced that our vice president, Chuck Jackson, and his staff would be coming to our office for our quarterly sales reviews. The formal review called for each salesperson to present their account penetration plan to the executive team. Shortly after the announcement, Ji-Yoon asked to meet with me privately. She informed me of a problem she had with addressing the executive team, especially senior male executives. Through this and other conversations, I gained more perspective on her background, which had contributed to her extreme nervousness in communication. For example, in the Korean business culture, women traditionally are seen as inferior to men. Coming from a family in which her father, a military officer, raised her under very strict conditions, her discomfort with speaking to the male executive team was understandable.

In fact, I initially suggested that she forgo the exercise if she did not want to do it. Despite her fears, however, she was insistent on giving it a try, which I found to be very courageous. To help control her anxious reactions, I suggested a few visualization and restructuring techniques, which she fully embraced.

One of the visual strategies was related to mentally seeing her presentation going well with great detail, including a positive outcome. Visualizing a positive ending was important because Ji-Yoon, like many others who struggle with these types of situations, had a tendency to mentally picture an unrealistic negative ending as inevitable. Science teaches us that these destructive thoughts are perpetuated through internal negative self-talk and beliefs. In addition, I also suggested that she do the same with other aspects of her presentation. Positive visualization helps calm these fears by reframing negative thoughts into positive, more realistic ones. Leading up to the presentation, Ji-Yoon worked hard on her talking points as well as on staying calm.

On the day of her presentation, she was well prepared. During her introduction, however, she was noticeably nervous, but she forged along and after a few minutes, seemed to be doing better. At the end of the presentation, as was the norm, the executives asked her questions. After fielding a few of them, she stopped and was suddenly overcome by emotion. I motioned to the group to allow her a few moments and to let her decide what should happen next. After gathering herself and making a brief apology, Ji-Yoon remained determined to finish her presentation. As she continued, her resolve became stronger and more determined. Eventually I could see that her emotions were at bay as she focused on her message. Although she had been shaken, something had changed in her forever.

Fast forward to the end of that fiscal year–Ji-Yoon's sales were among the best in the district and among the top performers in the country for her position. She told me that the experience with the executive team had helped her break through a barrier in her life. Ji-Yoon went on to build a successful sales career with Pitney Bowes and later in the corporate gifts industry, where she currently still works in sales. She also became a Toastmasters member, which further helped her conquer her fears and build her confidence. Ji-Yoon's story is an example of courage and resolve in dealing with *communication apprehension* (**CA**), a form of anxiety that involves a perceived fear of being judged during communications. At the moment of fight or flight, she decided to fight and learn to control her fears. That was over ten years ago, but these days Ji-Yoon's life is full of constant new challenges. But the more daunting the task, the more likely you'll find her right there, ready to take it on.

This story is perhaps a more extreme case of CA that few of us experience. But how do we deal with anxious feelings we all experience from time to time? For example, you feel anger or embarrassment when a prospect cuts you off or tells you that they are shopping your price. Whatever the reasons, the anxiety you feel could place you at a critical-decision crossroads. For those who sell by demonstrating their product, you've probably seen situations where something goes terribly wrong with the product during the demo. You feel the sweat building over your forehead and face as anxious thoughts fill your mind. You may decide to deal with the anxious feelings at that moment, at a later time, or ignore them altogether.

There are no single right answers, but self-awareness is the key to choosing the best path. When you become aware of your body's response to stress, you then have a chance to talk yourself down, if you will. Once you start to notice your triggers and reactions, you learn to stop CA before it can occur. This takes the element of surprise away, which happens to be one of its primary fuel sources. With improved understanding of potential anxious triggers, sellers can work toward eliminating them.

Effective communication is essential to sales success. However, as we learned with the previous story, emotions can arise that challenge us from reaching our full potential. For some, these feelings may even happen on routine calls. We all can sometimes feel a little nervous before a high-stakes sales call. But when these feelings begin to affect selling outcomes, they could be part of a larger underlying issue of CA. Note that CA in the selling context is different from a clinical anxiety disorder, which is a serious medical condition that can disrupt a person's quality of life. In such cases, one must seek professional medical attention. But CA in selling typically surfaces before and during sales interactions. It can cause varying degrees of problems to a seller's performance. Depending on how the sales interaction evolves, CA can dissipate or intensify. But there are different degrees of CA. So the important thing is to realize that it is natural and your goal is to keep it from affecting your performance.

Strategies for Controlling CA

When it comes to dealing with CA, the central goal is to control the anxious thoughts and find calmness. Humans have built-in psychological and physical reactions when we feel stressed. Sweat develops in the hands and other parts of the body as our heart rate increases. Our thoughts can become negative, making the feeling of uncertainty even worse. Many times, a person exhibiting CA may create unrealistic visions of failure in their mind, which distorts reality. So the question that many sellers ask is, "How can CA be mitigated to improve persuasive communication?" We address this question with two proven strategies:

1. Control Breathing
2. Visualization

Breathing is a natural act, but when CA strikes, it can be altered, setting off the chain reaction from the brain to the respiratory system.

We have all noticed breathing changes in ourselves or others in the midst of stress. A key action to managing CA is to recognize how your breathing pattern changes and try the following:

- Take long deep breaths
- Where appropriate, close your eyes and count to ten, twenty, or thirty
- Focus on re-establishing your normal breathing pattern

Try this test to better understand breathing and stress reactions: Breathe in and out slowly to a count of four seconds. Repeat several times until you form a pattern, then try to clench your jaw, teeth, hands, and arms; close your eyes tightly. You will notice that it is virtually impossible for your body to do all this at the same time. Regaining control of your breathing is a proven method for handling CA and other forms of stress.

As mentioned earlier, CA hijacks the seller's thoughts, falsely convincing them that they will fail at communication. The seller may have fears ranging from feeling uneasy about the interaction to being publicly humiliated. As you discovered in the case story, visual techniques help to counter these negative thoughts. Moreover, by using visualization regularly, you help shape your positive thoughts of self-concept and beliefs.

Some people naturally regard salespeople as extroverts who thrive on human interaction. But this is a myth. Consider that many people are drawn to sales because they want to get in the door of certain companies. Maybe they really want to be an engineer, but once out of college, they couldn't find the job they wanted. I have personally known many people who ended up in sales from this situation. It happens all the time. Thus, many introverts may find themselves in sales for different reasons. The better news is that people of all personalities perform well in sales. It should also be noted that CA can effect anyone, not just introverts.

Healthy Living and a Little R&R

Police officers, firefighters, and military personnel can face life-threatening situations while carrying out their duties—talk about the stress! Although in sales, we don't face these types of high-stakes situations, we have our share of stress and pressures in our work. With almost 40 percent of all salespeople not achieving sales quota, this means that many are not earning the income they need. Some are facing the possibility of losing their job due to performance. The harsh realities of having to make the sales quota every month and every year is always in the back of our minds. For many salespeople, these pressures can become overwhelming. Too many salespeople burn themselves out to the point of physical exhaustion. There's an old saying in sports: "Fatigue makes cowards of us all." Even the best can reach a point where they cannot function optimally when they become too stressed. Although life can sometimes create emotional stress with family or other personal matters, sellers must find ways to minimize these types of disruptions. Selling at an expert level requires a high level of focus and attention. And the reality is that sales organizations demand results, despite these personal distractions. Many companies offer medical benefits that provide support for family or personal issues. If you have a need and have access to these services, you should use them along with other resources.

As a salesperson, it is also important to watch your nutritional intake and maintain healthy eating habits. Most B2B sales reps drive around throughout the day, and it's very easy to grab unhealthy foods when you're on the go. This can be dangerous. Instead, bring a healthy lunch, or find healthier food from restaurants within your territory. By the way, I'm glad to share a little secret that helped me change my eating habits. The key word is *habits*. Recall my weight loss story? I decided to find a healthy low-calorie lunch that I enjoyed and just have it every day. For me that was my favorite wonton soup from a nearby restaurant. When you automate your good habits into a routine, they're much easier to maintain. After following the healthy lunch regimen for just a few days, you no longer have to worry about having the wrong thing for lunch. Of course, every once in a while, you can switch it up and have something a bit more filling or treat yourself to a tastier meal.

Make sure you're drinking enough water throughout the day as well. If you drive in warm climates or during the summer months, a good practice is to pack an ice cooler with bottles of water in your car. Another way to stay hydrated is to purchase cold water at a convenience store. For B2C retailers, coolers may work if you don't have access to a refrigerator. Most nutrition experts advise adults to drink at least eight eight-ounce glasses of water each day. Water is the ultimate hydrator and does wonders for the body and the mind.

Maintaining a healthier lifestyle involves more than just eating right and staying hydrated. Is also means staying active. Whether you go to the gym or just walk in the park or on a treadmill, movement is important to your overall health. The number one reason why we don't exercise is, you guessed it, time. But making time to stay active is an important goal, though not necessarily an urgent one. Activities such as exercising and relaxation are essential to our success, but they're often put off by other pressing tasks. Therefore, once you decide to change your health habits, the next step is to make it happen. How do you do that? You plan it! For example, schedule time to work out the same way you schedule customer appointments. The greater news is, once you plan the activity, it can quickly become a habit.

In sales, vacations tend to be difficult to take and enjoy. After all, your sales quota and customer needs do not take the vacation with you. But, by all means, take vacation at least once a year. I learned this the hard way. During one stretch in the mid-1990s, I did not take a vacation for nearly six years. This stretch ended up having a negative effect on my family. Thankfully, I was fortunate to recognize it in time to right the situation. Thus, it is important to unwind and refocus away from work. Take a vacation, or perhaps a day off, whenever you feel you need it. Trust me, you will be more productive when you return rested compared to continuing to press your mind and body when it's tired. All of the sales experts that I know personally live by this philosophy: Work hard, but when you rest, avoid working while you are off. In sales, this can sometimes be tough because of the concern about serving customers' needs while you are out. There are ways to handle this. Work with your manager to come up with a plan to cover your accounts while you are not at work. Talk to your customers beforehand and alert them of the dates you will not be available and what to expect.

Last, take some time each day for reflection. As my wife often tells me as she's heading off to her day spa…"I need some 'me' time!" The idea with *me time* is to find a relaxing place just to be you. This is a great time to reflect on your goals, the good things as well as the challenges you have faced. It doesn't have to take very long, but doing it regularly is important. Yoga is also a great activity for reflection and refocusing. For me, I meditate and pray. Whatever outlet you decide to use, make it yours and make it a habit. You will not only be less stressed and do better work, you'll feel better overall.

You may be thinking, *What does taking vacations and eating right have to do with selling improvement?* The truth is, a lot. I have seen firsthand how taking them for granted can lead to trouble on the job, including declines in performance. If you are a workaholic, that's OK, just take time for yourself and when you go on vacation, do not bring work with you. Moving to the next level in your career is about making sure that you're healthy, rested, and at your best.

Confidence: The Power of Believing

"To succeed in life, you need two things: ignorance and confidence."
—**Mark Twain**

Superman. That was the first word that came to my mind in 1992 when I met Mike McColgan in San Gabriel, California, at my new-hire sales training. Mike was a highly successful sales rep and perennial President's Club national-award achiever. I was new with Pitney Bowes, and Mike had been asked to address our new-hire class and share some tips on success. He entered the room wearing those classic horn-rimmed glasses like the character Clark Kent, and he stood well over six feet tall, hence the *Superman* tag. He spoke for about an hour, but I can sum up his message in one sentence: "Just believe that you can do it, and you will!" The class peppered Mike with questions on all kinds of topics, from territory management to how many diamonds were in his President's Club ring. But my memory of his greatest attribute was etched into my mind as soon as he walked into the room and began to speak: confidence. He simply exuded it, and it was contagious. I thought, *That's how you need to be in sales to command credibility and mutual respect, especially with C-level decision makers.*

From that point on, Mike and I developed a strong professional connection. When I took over the Southern California sales operation in 1998, he would stop by and we'd talk about selling. Those conversations provided valuable insights into Mike's expert selling style and confident mindset. I recall one situation where Mike was working with a large client in the energy industry. The buyer was considering replacing all of the mailing systems due to their age and growing downtime. However, the buyer wanted to phase in the replacements over a period of several years in order to ensure minimal disruptions to operations. After analyzing the plan, Mike realized that his customer would sacrifice significant productivity and other benefits if they waited until all of the machines needed to be replaced. Mike decided to craft a detailed implementation plan that would be completed in six months, thereby improving the customer's bottom line much sooner. The buyer agreed but only under the condition that Mike personally take full responsibility for the success of the plan.

That is when he went into action. He met with all involved stakeholders and laid out his plan. He met with the service management team, finance group, and the customer service department. All business functions were involved and organized to deliver what the customer needed. Although the schedule would be tight, Mike conveyed great confidence that everyone would succeed and deliver. Guess what happened? Everyone *did* deliver. And the customer was elated with the new systems and the benefits they received for their business almost immediately.

The following year at President's Club in Boca Raton, Florida, I played golf with Mike and I wondered if that confidence spilled over into his golf game. And sure enough, Mike Mc"Confidence" was just as sure of himself on the golf course. During a round of play, he approached a tee shot of about three hundred forty yards. Before taking the shot, he predicted that it would go just where he wanted. He took his swing, and it was a thing of beauty. Although it was a great-looking shot, it didn't go quite as straight as he had predicted. Mike's belief in himself was developed through his long career of success. He leveraged confidence to drive himself to higher heights and into becoming an expert salesperson. In a few years, Mike plans to retire where he can get a little more time out on the greens. And knowing Mike, I'm sure in no time he'll perfect that tee shot as well.

Self-confidence is often mistaken as arrogance or cockiness, but there is a distinct difference. Salespeople need confidence because customers tend to feel better about buying from people who believe in their product and themselves. If you are unsure of how your product can help your customer, this uncertainty can transmit doubt to the buyer. Expert sellers are confident in part because of their preparation and their personal experiences of providing value to customers.

In 1999, while in the district director role at Pitney Bowes, I hired a former top Xerox sales executive to my staff. Peter Rodarte had been a longtime Xerox sales rep selling high-ticket printer reproduction systems like the flagship DocuTech. A DocuTech could sell for several hundred thousand dollars per unit. When Peter joined us, our most advanced mailing product sold for about fifty thousand dollars. Since this product had strong similarities to the DocuTech system, Peter naturally gravitated toward it. When I saw his sales projections for the upcoming year, I was floored to see such large numbers for his unit projections. Most of my team had grown up in the industry where they only knew to sell one mailing machine to one customer at a time. Peter's idea of bundling multiple fifty-thousand-dollar units for a single transaction was unheard of to most of us at the time, but he believed he could do it, largely because he had already done it before in his career. Peter ended up selling those units like you'd sell bananas—in bunches! By the end of the year, he led the nation in sales for this product category and was one of the top specialists in the company. I learned something from Peter that I have kept with me ever since: When a person has great confidence, he or she can not only produce great individual results, but they also inspire others. A decade later that same inspiration led Peter and me to form Sales Development & Performance, where our mission is to inspire sales professionals to strive for expertise and excellence in all they do.

The way confidence works in the mind is an interesting phenomenon. If a person is not truly confident but can *act* confident, with time, the mind cannot detect the difference. Hence, the mind begins to send signals that instruct the person to exhibit confident behaviors. Before you know it, the person *acting* confident *is* confident. OK, I'll wait here while you go back and read those last couple of sentences again … It seems counterintuitive, but the mind tends to work that way. Therefore, if you feel a little apprehensive or nervous … fake it! At least until you don't need to anymore.

For decades, sports psychologists have used mind-control techniques to assist athletes with overcoming performance barriers in the most critical situations. In the book *Winning State-Football*, author Steve Knight suggests that athletes use the imagery of two distinct mindsets: the little dog and the BIG-Dog. The little dog has a doubtful mindset that says *can't do*, while the BIG-Dog's is often overconfident and focused on the wrong things. Therefore, the strategy is to set the conditions to control each mindset and manage the emotions accordingly. Although this analogy is from an athletic point of view, it is not very different from the confidence battles that sellers face every day. Controlling your thoughts and emotions is a key aspect of confidence. To be an expert, you must train your mind to believe in yourself and always be prepared to perform at your best.

Commitment to Continuous Learning

As a rookie sales manager in the early 1990s, I met Dick Franz, a longtime successful sales rep with the company. He had about thirty years' tenure at Pitney Bowes. Dick sold the old-fashioned way, using leverage and push tactics. Conversely, I was interested in all of the latest sales trends of the time. Dick was short, with a stocky build and the absolute jolliest smile. He was just a fun-loving guy who looked kind of like Santa Claus without the beard. He'd often come into my office to chat and share a bit of his philosophy. One morning I had finished delivering a training lesson to my team on consultative selling. Dick stopped by and asked what topic I had covered in training that day. "Retaining leasing customers using consultative selling skills," I said. He replied, "Well, I guess that's OK for the newbies, but I could have taught your class in five minutes on renewing customer leases. I'd just walk in and give 'em the same line I've been using for years." I reluctantly asked, "What's that, Dick?"

The following is the dialogue that Dick described:

Dick: "I got some good neeews and some bad neeews!"
Customer: 'What's the bad news?'
Dick: "You're gonna get a neeew mailing machine!"
Customer (stunned): "What's the bad news?"
Dick: "It's gonna cost you more money! So sign here because I need to get your paperwork in today."

The story is humorous, but it was also a stark reminder that Dick was not going to end up in any of my new-wave sales training classes. He was intent on retiring (which he did proudly) knowing just what he knew, which had worked for him most of his career.

I continued to share this story with many students over the years, where I'd say, "Don't be like Dick Franz." Then I'd quickly explain that while Dick was a successful sales rep for his time, eventually time caught up and passed him by. Therefore, never stop learning. Reaching your full potential requires lifelong learning and improvement.

Understanding the role of awareness of knowledge is key to personal growth. But how does learning differ in experts and novices? The answers lie in the application of the three stages of learning theory. Recall from earlier in this book the three stages of learning a new skill: (1) cognitive, (2) associative, and (3) autonomous. Lesser-skilled performers tend to stop learning once they have moved through the associative stage. Additional years of experience do not improve the specific skill beyond the satisfactory level of performance. Ericsson asserts that experts, on the other hand, counteract automaticity by developing progressively complex mental representations for higher performance, which in turn remain in the cognitive and associative stages. This theory sheds light on why so many top performers continue improving at a faster rate than other performers. Given today's high demands and rapidly changing sales climate, improvement is no longer a luxury, it's a necessity. As we learned from Dick Franz, many years ago sellers may have gotten away with doing things the same way but things are much different today.

Another lesson we must learn is not to approach learning and performance as mutually exclusive things. Learning is closely linked to performance. Although the right training program will likely require a time investment, it should be time well spent for improvement. Therefore training programs should be properly designed and targeted to produce a measurable result. Moreover, as you will discover in section three, implicit learning can occur through work when the right conditions are set. We'll also explore the role of everyday technology like smartphones which enable today's sellers to learn whenever they need to, thereby optimizing both learning and performance.

In sum, be a continuous learner and learn as you perform. Once you acquire new skills, continue to push the learning envelope higher to expand those skills to new heights. Learning is not an event but rather an ongoing commitment to improvement. Whether moving from novice to journeyman or journeyman to expert and beyond, you should always strive for more knowledge.

Experience versus Experiences

Please join me on a little math exercise to find out the amount of usable experience of a sales manager of twenty-five years. He has made thirteen thousand two hundred sixty sales calls during ride-alongs with sales reps. Therefore, he has over thirteen thousand experiences by which he's observed selling interactions. As a result, patterns within his brain are formed allowing him to match experiences. From these matches, he accesses lessons learned and new insights as he engages in current selling situations. A large segment of his more than thirteen thousand selling experiences forms as tacit knowledge. As he gains experience, more knowledge is deposited in the form of memory. Of course, he accesses this knowledge anytime, and the more he does, the more he learns from himself; and when he learns from himself, his knowledge grows even more. So how much usable experience would a twenty-five year sales expert have? The math might look something like this:

Average number of sales calls daily	4
Average number of selling days annually	X 252
Subtotal	= 1008
Number of years selling	X 25
Total estimated number of sales calls	= 25,200

This salesperson has amassed over twenty-five thousand selling interactions over the course of his career. But what if he were also a passionate top performer with a mind to improve like LeBron James. When you look at his volume of experiences coupled with improvement, a picture of intuitive expertise emerges. This sales expert is none other than Ed Diba, whom you met in the introduction of this book.

Leveraging related knowledge and experiences are key factors in achieving expertise. Although many people accumulate years of experience, experience alone does not increase the accuracy of behaviors nor is it related to higher levels of performance. Thus, leveraging your experiences into useful knowledge is an important aspect of skill improvement and expertise. Throughout the rest of this book, we will discuss new ways to leverage experience into advanced skill.

Performance Goals: You Can't Achieve What You Can't See

In sales, we are used to goals. After all, most of us have a sales goal affectionately known as the *quota*. But there are many types of goals.

Psychologists widely acknowledge the following three-category goal system, as shown in (Table 4.1).

Table 4.1 Types of Performance Goals

Goal Type	Description	Examples
Outcome goals (results)	Goals designed to achieve an end result (comparative to others)	Make President's Club Earn $100,000 Sell $5 million
Performance goals (mastery)	Goals focused on self-improvement and are within your control (compare to self)	Improve close rate Improve presentation skills Improve listening skills
Process goals	Goals focused on improving skill processes that you must execute to achieve performance goals	"Speak in pictures" for clarity Allow customer time to reflect after key benefit is presented Summarize to make sure customer needs are understood

Many salespeople don't create their own goals in part because their employer sets quotas and other metrics for them. Top sales performers, on the other hand, have a set of goals aside from company-provided ones. The ideal goal-setting method is to first set your outcome goals, and then align your performance and process goals. For example, if your outcome goal is to increase sales by 15 percent for a new widget, you would then analyze the actions needed to determine performance goals. The process goals should represent subtasks of the overall performance goal. You can identify process goals by thinking through the actions within a skill and breaking them down into smaller steps. For instance, if the performance goal is to improve your close rate to 25 percent, the following process goals might be considered:

- Improve questioning for new widget
- Master widget product knowledge
- Interview and learn from other users of the widget

Performance goals should always stretch above your current performance level. It's also a good idea to monitor your progress and make adjustments as needed. A performance goals' skill inventory list can be found in Chapter 10; see Table 10.2. Use this template to write down your performance goals after you have created them.

In conclusion, you must take the time to master yourself before mastering skills. Your self-concept, which is how you view yourself, guides your thoughts and actions and is the genesis of self-confidence. Therefore, it is wise to feed your mind positive thoughts while avoiding negative inputs. Living a healthy, purposeful lifestyle is largely driven by your thoughts and beliefs of who you are. As such, the road to selling expertise begins between the ears.

Summary and Reflections on Section 1

How are we doing so far? We are nearly halfway through our journey! Before we move on, I think now might be a good time for a quick pit stop. Section one's mission was to understand the mindset and foundations of expert performance and how science has illuminated the pathway to selling expertise. In Chapter 1, "Connecting," we explored the research principles of recognition and how it applies to professional selling. These theories included intuitive decision making and the RPD model as well as situation awareness. Finally, we defined connecting as a form of recognition that sellers use to detect and react to prospect messages. Chapter 2's "Situation Selling" was a discussion of intuitive expertise used in common selling situations. Several case story examples were provided to connect situation expertise to real-world selling. A key takeaway from Chapter 2 is the importance of aligning the sales message to the buyer's needs. By recognizing key selling predicaments, salespeople can expand knowledge and pattern recognition, which advances intuitive skills.

In Chapter 3, "The Anatomy of Expert Sales Performance," we discovered the links between a seller's capability (KSAs), performance, and results. We also discussed tacit knowledge and its role in intuitive expertise. Finally, we were introduced to deliberate practice, a research-based training activity widely held as the component most responsible for the acquisition of expert performance. Chapter 4's "Expert Attitude and Self-Awareness" inventoried the mindset attitudinal qualities required to move from journeyman to expert. Part of this mindset involves the concept of self-awareness and a commitment to learning.

Section one laid the groundwork for discerning selling expertise and intuitive selling. We now move on to examine persuasive communication, which is how we express sales recognition abilities. Our aim in section two is to discover how to expertly communicate with buyers during sales interactions.

MASTERING THE SELLING ESSENTIALS: BECOMING BRILLIANT AT THE BASICS

Chapter 5

THE SIX ESSENTIALS OF PERSUASIVE COMMUNICATION

n section one, we discovered that intuitive sales ability is driven by improving the cognitive aspects of selling. We will draw from these foundational principles throughout the rest of the book. But the mind alone is incapable of selling, which raises these important questions: How do experts express this intuitive knowledge while selling? What do they know and do different than others that results in their superior performance? If you were a fly on the wall, watching a top sales performer in action, what skills would you see? In this section, we will discover answers to these questions as we break down the "Six Essentials of Persuasive Communication" (PC).

The Six Essentials of PC are effective planning, leveraging pause (and silence), presenting with clarity, attentiveness, perceptiveness, and responsiveness. The first three—planning, pausing, and clarity—

represent the *action* skills (behavioral expressive), which focus on the preemptive tasks of the seller. The other three essentials— attentiveness, perceptiveness, and responsiveness—reflect the *reaction* (cognitive-intuitive) skills of *connecting*. These represent the perceptual skills in selling. Therefore, connecting involves implicit learning of detecting meaningful nonverbal cues such as tone and body language, interpreting what is being expressed, and adapting messages that are well timed and appropriate for the situation.

Most people assume that top performers have special talents or abilities that account for their high level of skill. However, studies on expertise suggests that expert performance lies largely in performing routine tasks faster and more accurately than others. For example, in 2006, Mark Endsley conducted a study using pilot simulation tests and discovered that expert pilots didn't make better decisions than novices, but they were much faster and precise in making routine decisions and taking action. Hence, selling expertise is marked by exemplary performance of the six essentials that reflect the most basic skills in selling. Before we discuss each of these skills directly, let's take a look at a case story that exemplifies the broader aspects of sales communication along with some of the foundational research that validate these skills in selling.

Persuasive Skills – From Courtrooms to Boardrooms

Imagine this: you are trying to sell a product to a buyer, but they're not allowed to respond or speak back to you. And imagine that before you can even present your product, the competitor is allowed to present the buyer with a preponderance of reasons why they should not buy your product. Now envision a situation where the buyer first meets you with a predetermined bias that your product couldn't possibly be of use to them. If it's easy for you to imagine these scenarios, or maybe you encounter them on a daily basis, you're probably a defense trial attorney.

Trial attorneys know firsthand the importance of persuasive communication. Think about it; when a public defender typically gets a case, it's almost always a bleak situation from the onset. The police, generally highly regarded as community servants, have provided a report that is the first of a thorough list of evidence used to implicate the accused. Then the district attorney evaluates the police report and determines whether laws were broken and what criminal charges will be filed. Keep in mind that much or all of this usually takes place before a defense attorney ever takes the case.

No one is more familiar with this legal playing field than Rudolph "Rudy" Rousseau, who serves as a division chief with the Los Angeles County Public Defender's Office. Some people incorrectly assume that all public defenders are somehow less capable than private attorneys. But Rudy leads a team of bright talented lawyers who are regarded as some of the best legal minds in the criminal justice system. For an example of this legal expertise, look no further than the case in the following story that Rudy himself argued during his time as a public defender trial lawyer.

"Where's Ronny?" That was the question Rudy continued to ask throughout the trial of Benny Caldwell, who was accused and charged with attempted burglary and assault with a deadly weapon. When Rudy first reviewed the case, the prosecutors had built what looked to be an air-tight case. They had police reports and police statements supporting the alleged guilt of Mr. Caldwell. And they had Mr. Caldwell's background. Although he had not been convicted of a serious crime, the list of his numerous encounters with law enforcement painted a questionable picture of his character.

The case centered on a situation between Mr. Caldwell and his friend Ronny's girlfriend, Rhonda, who had called 911 to report a break-in and robbery. She reported that three men wearing masks (allegedly including Mr. Caldwell) broke into her home and took valuables while brandishing a pistol at her. Although she was not physically injured, the event left her traumatized psychologically.

Once assigned the case, Rudy's first order of business after discovery was to plan his strategy by formulating a defensive theory about the case. Many novice defense attorneys wait for the prosecution's case to be revealed, and then they react to it. But expert trial attorneys actually develop a theory of what happened—who did it—then argue their case versus simply reacting to the state's case. This forces the prosecution to deny the theory, which in effect places them in a defensive posture. Rudy explains that this is critical in a courtroom because jurors naturally want to blame someone for a crime, especially when committed against an innocent victim.

Given the fact that jurors are prohibited from speaking to attorneys, Rudy's next planning action was to anticipate every possible question a juror might be thinking, and answer them in his arguments. Questions like: who did it, why do the police think he did it, and so on.

Mr. Caldwell explained the incident to Rudy as a staged hoax concocted by Ronny to get back at his girlfriend, Rhonda, for cheating on him. He said that Ronny asked him and two other neighborhood friends to stage a break-in and to "scare the crap out of her." But when Rhonda began screaming, all three of the men ran away. Unfortunately, for Mr. Caldwell, his fingerprints were found at the scene and ultimately matched to his non-violent arrest record. The case would be won or loss based on which of the competing stories the jury ultimately believed.

When the trial began, Rudy noticed that one very important witness was nowhere to be found: Ronny. When asked why Ronny was not in the courtroom, Rhonda claimed that she didn't know. Rudy had a hunch that something was up so he pressed the issue. Not knowing if Ronny would show on the next day of court, he continued to ask: "Where's Ronny?" The next day came and went then the days turned to weeks, and still, no Ronny. Rudy built his case theory by using the theme "Where's Ronny," along with his top three answers to what he believes are the jurors' most pressing questions. These questions were addressed during the opening statement, trial arguments, and finally, in the closing argument.

As the trial moved on, the jury connected with Rudy's argument through his use of stories and the power of silence. One example was a true story about his grandfather who once taught him a memorable lesson about the value of your word. The story was riveting and culminated with a teachable moment for Rudy when his grandfather explained why a poor man who borrowed money from him worked for nearly a year to finally repay the debt. When the man made his last payment on the loan, he said: "All a man has is his word…thank you for allowing me to keep my word and my dignity." Rudy now turned to the jury, looked them directly in the eye, and said: "Ladies and gentlemen, Ronny is not perfect. He may have done some not-so-good things in his past, but like the poor man in the story, sometimes all a person has is their word." The deafening silence in the courtroom proved that Rudy's argument had resonated.

Another powerful aspect of persuasive communication is to invoke high-impact emotional language to connect with your audience's emotions. For example, a novice lawyer might cross-examine a crime scene investigator's sloppy work as: "Isn't it true Officer Jones, that you didn't use gloves when you collected that sample?" But the expert adds: "Officer Jones, isn't it true that as a public servant of the community, you jeopardize the freedom of an innocent taxpaying citizen when you don't do your job properly? And isn't it also true that this type of incompetence is outrageous and damages the trust of the very community you are sworn to serve?"

Although juries don't speak verbally with attorneys during trial, expert attorneys use connecting skills to interpret the jury's nonverbal messages and adopt the correct response. Rudy cites that his best attorneys can typically spot the foreman or key influencers of the jury based on these nonverbal cues. In many ways, because jurors don't speak, it can actually be easier to pick up signals of discontent, agreement, and so on from their nonverbal reactions.

In the end, the jury found Mr. Caldwell not guilty. Throughout the trial, Rudy continued to ask: "Where's Ronny?" At some point, the courtroom audience and even some jurors would finish Rudy's sentence as he repeatedly asked the rhetorical question. In his closing argument, Rudy asked the question once again and then finally answered it. "Maybe Ronny's not here because he doesn't want to explain why he had his 'boys' break into his girlfriend's house and pretend to rob her because he wanted to teach her a lesson. Maybe Ronny's not here because he would have to look his friend and girlfriend in the eye and explain where he was during this incident."

In many ways, the Caldwell case embodies the epitome of persuasive communication expertise. Although the context is a criminal trial, there are undeniable similarities to selling. In fact, the underlying communication skills are essentially the same. Expert communicators *plan* their communication with precise detail, use *pauses and silence* as a powerful tool to engage their audience, communicate with optimal *clarity*, and use connecting skills to better *detect*, *interpret*, and *respond* to their audience. Like a public defender, selling can often be an uphill battle to overcome predetermined biases of buyers. Successful sellers must develop expert level defense lawyer communication skill to the point where if your prospect is unable to speak to you, they'd still be compelled enough to buy from you.

The Role of Communication in Sales Performance

Communication expert D.J. Cegala defines **interactive involvement** as "the extent in which an individual partakes in a social environment." The broad components of interactive involvement include attentiveness, perceptiveness, and responsiveness (connecting). Within this framework, selling expertise is built implicitly using these three-dimensional skills. Throughout PC, salespeople are exposed to key messages that have the potential to shape the sale. Connecting allows you to turn recognized information into useful insights. It should be noted that developing connecting skills is not about specific ways to respond to prospects because experts often produce different decisions and solutions. We are more concerned with demystifying the *locations* of the expert advantage. The idea is that once you know where to focus your attention, your Spidey-sense can take over.

Selling involves many aspects of communication, including listening, understanding, speaking, reading, and writing. The ability to communicate well is central to excellent sales performance. During PC, sellers express their knowledge and value through messages sent to the prospect. Moreover, the expert seller expands these skills to include perceptual reactions to the prospect's messages. Research and objective review support the notion that salespeople offer the unique ability to create and modify custom messages. For instance, a 1998 study on relational communication concluded that **communication apprehension** (**CA**) and **interaction involvement**, play integral roles in adaptiveness and sales performance. The lower the apprehension and the better the involvement, the better the overall communication.

Adaptive selling is a sales strategy that focuses on adjusting the product or service message based on the prospect's buying criteria. It is widely held as a key ingredient of effective direct selling. Empirical studies have suggested that adaptive selling plays a significant role in selling outcomes. This is especially evident in high-value sales such as business technology or high-end retail. Sales researcher Barton Weitz defines adaptive selling as "the altering of sales behaviors during a customer interaction or across interactions based on perceived information on the nature of the selling situation." For years, sales thought leaders and researchers have searched for the answer to this simple question: "What role do communication skills play in sales results?"

In "Adaptive Selling and Sales Performance: An Empirical Examination," an important 2000 landmark sales study, researchers found strong links to adaptive selling and sales performance outcomes. While this study and others are not always 100 percent conclusive, they reveal meaningful insights on the link between adaptive selling and sales outcomes. But, putting aside all the research data, we can make the more practical argument that:

1. The act of selling is fundamentally executed using communication skills.
2. A salesperson's primary function is to convey product and service messages based on the buyer's unique needs and buying requirements.

This naturally leads us to the priorities of PC and adaptive selling as the catalyst for advancing intuitive selling skill.

Most salespeople naturally develop their own unique structure of communication, such as speech patterns and reactions. Some might use a quick speaking pace that sounds excited and upbeat, whereas others may speak using a more even-toned, methodical pace. The purpose of this discussion isn't to recommend a particular style or process, but rather to suggest that you notice the prospect's (and your own) communication patterns. By identifying these patterns, structures, and tendencies, you are better positioned to adapt your message to the prospect's style and preferences.

Personality-Style Models

What if you went into your favorite supermarket or department store only to find that all the products were randomly shelved without any categories? Given the plethora of products, brands, and sizes we have to choose from, we can all imagine that this would be a nightmare shopping experience. When we look at human behaviors and personalities, there are many variations that make it more difficult to organize people as well. Rather than try to analyze all the personal attributes of every prospect, it's much easier to identify certain style indicators. These indicators can be quickly categorized into a predominant style for most people.

Personality-style modeling is well established and widely accepted theory within psychological and academic circles worldwide. As a result, there are many personality and style assessments that are available today. Most of these tests categorize personal styles into four or five groups. For instance, the DiSC profile assessment uses four categories: "D" for dominant, "I" for influence, "S" for steadiness, and "C" for conscientious. A dominant person is task driven and decisive in their actions. Notable examples of high D's include Vince Lombardi and Margaret Thatcher. An influencer is marked by persuading others to work with them to achieve a common goal. Salespeople in general tend to fall into the influence group and there are notable influencers such as former US President Bill Clinton and television host and author Katie Couric. People who are profiles in steadiness are good team players and tend to work well with others to achieve common goals. Mother Teresa and legendary journalist Charlie Gibson are examples of the "S" profile. Finally, people who are conscientious are procedure driven and analytical and they focus on accuracy and detail. Star Trek's Mr. Spock character as well as Bill Gates represent the "C" profile. The DiSC profile system, as with most others, allows for a balance between the categories. Although some people will come out mainly in one category, others, including myself, tend to fall within multiple groups. For instance, I'm a "low D" "high I," which is described as an assertive person capable of direct, dynamic action or charming sociability as the situation demands.

Generally, the DiSC as well as other personality assessments provide insights on how to best identify and adapt to different communication styles. The central idea is based on the truism: *The better you know yourself, the better you can understand others.* Personality tests can be helpful to salespeople in part because they provide a logical framework by which to organize thoughts and patterns more quickly. Said another way, knowledge and memory of personality styles can speed up recognition. While there are many good personality assessments and tests available today, the following offer specific models that are geared toward sales or communication:

- DiSC Profile (*www.discinsights.com*)
- The Social Styles Model (*www.wilsonlearning-americas.com*)
- Neuro Linguistic Programming (NLP) (*www.nlp-mentor.com*)

Essential #1: Brilliant Planning

Depending on the sales role and industry, planning activities may require as much as 20 percent or more of the seller's time. Before an important meeting, most people tend to engage in some sort of preparation. Salespeople usually prepare in advance of product demos and other critical sales activities. So when it comes to planning for your sales presentations, you should prepare with the same level of fervor. Any good planning process should include thinking through the prospect's situation and devising a message that is well organized to achieve their goals. PC planning serves several purposes, one of which is to reduce the effects of CA. Within sales communication, CA has been found to be most responsible for ineffective communication. PC planning allows you to preview your message in a non-selling environment, thereby reducing nervousness.

Predictability is one of the great opponents of CA. When you prepare, you worry less about what could go wrong. Therefore, another aim of planning is to build confidence. When you're able to think through your dialogue and map out your presentation, you become more self-assured of your plan and your delivery. Planning on the surface may seem time consuming, but in fact it is a highly productive act. The key is to make your PC planning part of your normal planning activities.

Although time is thought to be the biggest reason why salespeople fail to plan, ego and past success take a close second. There are those who fall into the trap of thinking that they can just show up and wing it. Seasoned experts, on the other hand, leave nothing to chance. Even though they may be good enough to wing it, they don't.

Visualization and Mental Rehearsal

As a high school football player, I was introduced to visualization for the first time. Mrs. Ye, our math teacher, met with the team every Thursday to lead us through visualization for Friday night's game. We would huddle on the gym floor with the lights turned off, and she would help us visualize ourselves succeeding in the game. Each player would envision key plays and situations that he could face on Friday night and mentally execute his performance. By the end of the session, the team felt confident, ready, and even anxious to get on the field and play. And more often than not, the team's mental focus was improved and primed for game situations.

The following information describes how many sales experts use visual techniques as mental rehearsals to prepare for key presentations. First, imagine the dialogue exchange in your head, including the anticipated responses of the prospect. See yourself smiling and looking confident, which tends to bring more reality to the process. On the day and time of the actual presentation, you will feel confident because you've already performed the task in your mind. The actual interaction then becomes the act of fulfilling the moment that already exists in your head.

Visual techniques are encouraged by many sports psychologists and communication experts. Studies also suggest that these techniques can encourage or help CA. For example, in Michael L. Boorom's 1998 study on sales communication, he stated, "Higher levels of CA stem from excessive visualization of pathetic attempts to communicate and unreasonable expectations about communication outcomes." So negative visuals tend to increase CA whereas positive ones can reduce it. Visualization can replace negative images with positive ones by concentrating on a "so far so good" approach that breaks the overall presentation into a series of steps. Looking ahead enhances sales planning by creating a mental roadmap to success. Training your mind to preview your presentation can reduce CA and thereby increase cognitive focus on the prospect. While visualizing represents planning of the mind, routine preparation is also an important part of sales planning.

Planning the Sales Meeting Structure

A few years ago, I joined a sales team member on a sales call at a large San Diego biotech firm. As the sales rep presented his proposal, the customer became confused. It was clear from her puzzled look that she had no idea how the product would help her business. After the call, I asked the rep why he hadn't mentioned how the product would fit into the customer's requirements. His response was, "I did—when I met with her on the first call." The problem was, that first meeting had taken place nearly a month before.

Part of PC expertise is repeating yourself without sounding repetitive. It is important for salespeople to develop a clear narrative of the prospect's needs, and then drill it home with each interaction. For example, you can get the prospect to reinforce the clarity of needs by asking them to express how they see the solution meeting their needs or goals.

Another common error involves starting a meeting without giving a recap of the previous discussions or background information. It's as if we assume the prospect has been lying awake at night since our last meeting, thinking about our product or service. Obviously, this is not the case. It is important therefore to recap early in the selling interaction. This sets the table for what is to come.

Many sellers create confusion for the buyer by jumping around throughout the presentation. Customers often become frustrated when the sales dialogue becomes choppy and disjointed. If you were reading a book that randomly jumped around to different paragraphs, you probably wouldn't enjoy the book very much. A sales interaction should flow like a well-written story in the sense that each line connects throughout the book. At times, a prospect will derail your meeting structure (usually unintended). This is where many abandon the meeting structure as a result. Adjusting and adapting to the prospect does not mean winging your presentation. If a prospect gets you off track, it is important to get back on course as soon as possible. You should also use the meeting structure notes from your computer, tablet, or smartphone or even a hard copy during the meeting. This way, if you get off track, you can see where you left off and resume the presentation from there. Some sellers push back on using notes during PC, arguing that they may be perceived as inexperienced. My response comes in the simple analogy of air travel: "We've all flown on an airplane where the cockpit door is sometimes opened before takeoff. You see the pilot and copilot going through the preflight checklist. But ask yourself, would you want to fly with the pilot that just sort of *tries to remember* most of the items from the checklist?" I'm sure you wouldn't and fortunately for those of us who fly, the FAA doesn't allow this to happen anyway.

In addition, most prospects appreciate a well-organized meeting because they want to be as productive as possible. A well-planned meeting helps to guide PC to the desired goal as well as reveal repeatable patterns.

These patterns allow for easier improvements such as pinpointed error detection and format adjustments. Said another way, if you randomly run meetings differently each time, it's much harder to find out which parts aren't working.

The main purpose of the meeting structure is to provide organization to the interaction and to optimize PC effectiveness. A well-planned meeting doesn't create a canned feel but rather it should foster a natural dialogue that achieves the PC goals. Consider the following format to guide your customer meetings:

Suggested Customer Meeting Format
1. Introduction, opening, and pleasantries
2. Meeting goals or purpose and overview of prospect benefits (or potential benefits)
3. Recap of previous meeting or background situation
4. Topic 1 (should be the most logical to come first)
5. Topic 2 (should be next most logical)
6. Topic 3 (should be next most logical) and so on (Try limiting to three-four topics)
7. Summary (recap of key points and prospect needs)
8. Follow-up, next steps, scheduling

It is important to note that planning your meeting structure does not impede flexibility of reacting to the prospect. Selling is not a linear process; it's a dynamic human interaction requiring agility and flexibility. However, the meeting structure provides a track to guide the dialogue to its defined goals. When we just go with the flow, we often create unnecessary confusion for the prospect, which decreases the odds for success. For B2B sellers, who often make several calls during the sales cycle, maintaining clarity throughout is critical.

Planning the Sales Presentation

Now that we have laid out the structure of the meeting, let's take a look at how we plan and execute our presentation content. When it comes time to presenting your product solution, your presentation skills play a significant role in the outcome of the sale. The first step in the process is to prepare an outline. The outline is a roadmap that fits within the framework of the meeting structure that we just discussed. It includes the key talking points, organized into a logical list of topics that you plan to cover. While there are many sales presentation outlines to choose from, consider the following basic elements:

- A compelling opening. The opening should include a scripted dialogue focused on the solution benefits that directly link to the customer's unique needs.
- A clear main theme. This is the essence of the value proposition. It is a brief synopsis of the customer's primary goals or needs and how your product solution answers them.
- The close. The seller makes a conclusive case for the prospect to purchase by summarizing the key presentation points and giving compelling reasons to act now.

These outline elements may seem a bit elementary, and they are. But let's face it, we know a lot more than we do. The key is not just knowing … but doing.

Identifying a central theme that drives the sale is a critical task within sales planning. Targeted questions are used to qualify and uncover key needs and the buying objectives of the prospect. Typically, these needs are matched with the seller's product or service, and a proposal is created for the buyer's consideration. The problem with this approach is that the seller often does not clearly articulate the prospect's objectives. Buyers must understand the clear compelling reasons they should take action.

Many times sellers, after gathering information from the prospect, will (internally) interpret the feedback and develop a proposal. But when this work is done in a vacuum, the prospect may not be clear on the rationale for the solution. Thus, when the salesperson later presents her solution, it's often much more difficult to justify the price.

After preparing your outline, it is time to structure the opening of the presentation. Patricia Fripp, a recognized expert on sales presentation and communication skills, suggests that salespeople script the opening and closing of their presentations. She also advocates prerecording presentations for perfect delivery. Your opening should emphasize the central theme of the sale and be packaged in a compelling statement that resonates with the prospect. This statement should also define the vision of the sale in terms of the projected measurable benefits of your product.

For instance, a manufacturer's rep selling circuit boards might open with, *"Today you can leverage our technology to meet your JIT (just in time) distribution objectives while reducing inventory related costs by 30 percent. We deliver this value through our vast network of manufacturer relationships, which enable you to achieve the right product for the right customer at the right price."* The central theme is underlined and the overall opening statement sets a clear vision of the goal for the sale. Next comes the body of the presentation, which features the key problems or objectives and how your solution will solve those needs. Each section of the presentation is presented in order of importance and priority for the prospect. The talking points for the body presentation should be stated in clear language that links the business issue to the problem and your product solution. Pricing and terms should follow while questions may come throughout the presentation or at the end of the discussion. Once all questions have been addressed, it is time for the summary conclusion.

The best thing I can tell you about the conclusion is to simply do it last. One notable example of the consequences of failing to close meetings with a strong summative conclusion involves fielding questions from the prospect. Many salespeople make the mistake of concluding their presentation and then dealing with questions at the end. After answering the questions, the meeting ends. This is dangerous for several reasons. First, the impact of the sales presentation is either lost or greatly diminished after a round of questions and answers. Questions are important and must be addressed before asking for a commitment.

The seller must end by delivering a high-impact, conclusive statement that reinforces how the solution solves the buyer's problems. Second, the conclusion must include compelling reasons for the prospect to act now. A general rule in selling is that when you present, you should expect to close. It is important to always ask the prospect for the commitment to do business regardless of whether you're expecting to receive the order. The key action is to demonstrate clear, compelling reasons why the prospect should purchase *your* product. When the presentation ends on a strong closing statement, you increase the odds of shaping what the prospect remembers.

Influencers are not the ultimate decision makers, but when prepared properly, they can drive buying decisions just as well. In many cases, the person receiving the presentation is an influencer and must present the proposal to other decision makers. You want influencers to know the key talking points of your value proposition, as well as the benefits and advantages. As a result, when presenting to an influencer, the presentation should be adjusted to coach the influencer on how to present to the decision maker. For example, when presenting to an influencer, you'll want to include well-written materials and clear and concise visual aids. The central goal is to make the influencer an informed sponsor that knows the value proposition and can sell it to others.

During the actual presentation, you will also want to have a winning structure for presenting the features of your product. There are plenty of models from which to choose. The *FAB* (**feature, advantage, and benefit**) format still works for some product-oriented sales.

Many companies have also developed their own presentation models. Regardless of the presentation tools you use, be sure to use a structured process that organizes your deliverables while providing overall clarity.

To sum up, an effective presentation structure should include a compelling opening that helps to level-set the discussion and establish the PC goals that resonate long after the meeting. The central themes encapsulate the value proposition and provide clarity. A compelling close summarizes the solution while creating urgency for the buyer to take action.

Essential #2: Brilliant Pause and Silence

If you want to get a glimpse into the awesome power of communication expertise, look no further than to the late author, poet, and professor Dr. Maya Angelou. I was struck by the way she could take just a few words and literally change people's lives. Most of us naturally ascribe Maya's gift of eloquence to the fact that she was a poet and scholar; but when you really listened to her speak, what you did *not* hear was equally important. At times, she abruptly ended a sentence or phrase and waited until the right time to continue. Other times she applied pauses in between words, which seemed to invoke a unique meaning and interpretation of her message. The use of pausing and silence was an unsung key to her uncanny ability to resonate with people from all walks of life. Listeners had time to not only think about Maya's words, but many believed that they could *feel* them as well. There are many other examples of great communicators who leverage pausing. Their voices command attention yet they do not shout or try to squeeze in the most words. Although brief silence may not be the sexiest part of communication, like breathing is to life, pausing is an essential element of PC excellence.

There's a truism in selling that says, "After you've asked for the order, the first one who speaks loses." Obviously, this is not an absolute, but there's merit in knowing when to stop talking and allow time for making a decision. In certain scenarios, a few seconds of pause can achieve greater feats than even the most eloquent words. Pausing is an essential element of effective communication for several reasons. First, a pause provides a clear opportunity for the other person to speak. Many times the buyer has a contributory thought or objection that never gets heard. Recall in Chapter 1, implicit concerns that go undetected oftentimes can become *surprise* objections later in the sales cycle. Second, a pause reduces communication "noise," allowing each party time to absorb the message.

As conversations extend longer, uninterrupted dialogue can lead to distractions such as boredom or topic jumping. Pausing allows time for the buyer to speak and provide feedback, which increases their engagement. Noise on the other hand often robs communication of its intent and clarity. Third, longer pauses allow time for reflection, which encourages mental concentration and careful consideration. As such, both buyers and sellers are more likely to intuitively connect with messages.

Sellers often fail to pause when they are excited about strong buying signs. Notable signals for this heightened excitement level may include a faster speech pace or a sudden change in voice tone. Before you know it, very few commas and periods are acknowledged, if at all. One of the common errors of failing to pause occurs during joint calls with a sales manager. For instance, the manager makes a salient point to the prospect, but the salesperson immediately jumps in and makes a different point. Often times, the initial statement is drowned out when the buyer is distracted. This type of impromptu interjection usually succeeds in diminishing message clarity, which can hinder the sale. But the most common violation of pausing occurs when a prospect is speaking and the salesperson interrupts them. This is almost always unacceptable, but sadly, it happens way too often. In fairness, it is usually unintentional.

Perhaps the salesperson starts to hear a question or concern that he is ready to answer, so he impulsively interrupts the prospect. If only salespeople could notice the prospect's facial and body language when this happens, the problem could be fixed promptly. The good news is that later in this section, we will explore nonverbal connecting, which allows you to do just that. But our focus at the moment is on how to avoid triggering these concerns and giving them legs to walk.

If you're concerned with forgetting pertinent information during conversations, try jotting down a quick note and waiting until the buyer completes his thought. A top sales expert once said that she waits until she hears the period at the end of the buyer's sentence, and as a result, she rarely misses an objection. Failing to use pausing can inhibit your overall selling effectiveness. While pausing is naturally learned over time, these skills can also be intentionally improved through routine conversations.

Pausing can be improved through practice during discussions as well as nonselling conversations. For example, you can observe yourself and others while engaged in business conversations. Notice if both parties easily convey their points and whether ample time is allowed for reflection. Finally, pay attention to whether the message was understood from each person's point of view.

Choose *and* instead of *but*. At times, prospects will make statements and nonverbal cues that may be perceived as a potential threat to the sale. In these cases, the natural response is to interject with the word *but*. This word suggests that the message sent was rejected or not fully received. An alternative word to use in the place of *but* is *and*. I am always amazed how such a small word can make such a big difference during conversations.

You can also leverage peer and supervisor feedback to improve the use of pausing. Many sales cultures foster ride-along days where peers or the sales manager make calls together. The following activities can be used to leverage others for skills practice:

1. Ask a peer or manager to observe your conversation pace, notate times where you pause and wait for feedback and times where you do not.
2. Ask the observer to note any instances where you cut off or interrupt the prospect during a conversation.
3. Ask the observer to evaluate the response to your pauses by the prospect. Do they chime in with their thoughts and feedback? Do they ask questions? Do they take the time to mull over the message? Use their feedback to find new insights that work to self-coach the use of pausing during PC.

Longer pauses become silence, which can be used in either positive or negative ways. Often, silence is leveraged to apply pressure to the buyer from the seller or vice versa. This pressure may be appropriate unless it's taken too far—to the point of manipulation or intimidation. When silence is used by a buyer or seller as a ploy to force an unwanted decision, it becomes a negative action.

Professionalism involves presenting a collaborative posture that is supportive and beneficial to both the buyer and the seller. Silence can be used in a positive way to convey empathy and genuine concern. For example, Steve Hart, whom you met in Chapter 2, would often use silence to ponder roadblocks or an obstacle introduced by the prospect. Prospects appreciated the fact that Steve took time to consider their problem as if it were his own. Oftentimes, prospects think of a work-around in the middle of the silence.

Many sellers also use silence during price and terms negotiations. When a prospect requests a concession, you want to be very thorough in your thinking. In this context, use silence to create time to examine the concession's implications before responding. You may not always make the concession right then, but you afford yourself more time to decide *when* to decide.

Essential #3: Brilliant Clarity

One of my longtime practices as a sales manager was to randomly call sales prospects from my team's sales pipeline. My goal was to try to determine what I could do to assist customers in making their decision. I'd block off a window of time each week, pull out the list, and start dialing. Inevitably, as I would speak to influencers and decision makers, certain common themes would emerge that gave me new insights into the prospect's understanding of our offer. Table 5.1 depicts the flow of one of these typical phone conversations.

Table 5.1 Typical Dialogue Flow Between Sales Manager and Prospect

Item	Speaker	Example Dialogue
1	Manager	Hi, this is Sedric Hill. I'm the sales manager here at XYZ. First of all, thank you for your business/consideration. I understand you've been working with John, who handles your account. I'm calling to follow up and see if there's anything I can do or if you have any outstanding questions that I can answer.
1a	Prospect	Yeah, we are looking at [acquiring, upgrading, adding, etc.] our system. We haven't had much time to get into it because things have been really busy.
2	Manager	Yes, I understand—seems there's never enough time in the day. Let me ask you, has John provided you everything you need to make a good decision? What do you like most about the proposal? Can you see how the [product or feature] will … [whatever the product or feature is designed to do]?
2a	Prospect	Well, actually, that's one of the questions I have. Hold on, let me look at it [*getting the proposal*]. What exactly does this [product or feature] do? I'm not sure we need that part.
3	Manager	I'll be glad to answer those questions for you. [*Answers questions.*] Would you like me to ask John to contact you to get everything started for you?
3a	Prospect	Yes, that'll be fine. Thank you.

During items 2a and 3 is when I would often discover that the customer did not have a good understanding of our offer nor the benefits of the product. During item 3, I would try to clarify and refresh the main benefits of the presentation in two or three key points. Many times, this would help rekindle the interest in our offer, giving the sales rep a stronger chance of success. Other times, the call would reveal that the sale was actually already dead. In either case, the question that we must address is, "Why do prospects lose clarity and get lost in the sales messaging?" You might assume that the salesperson was not doing his or her job of making calls, but that assumption has proven not to be the case. For instance, I typically would ask the prospect how the sales rep was doing in terms of following up and being responsive to their needs. In most cases, there were no issues with the salesperson; yet the prospect remained unclear on the reasons they should buy.

My hypothesis as to the cause of this fuzziness is twofold: (1) The salesperson did not communicate with clarity, and as a result, the prospect is unclear on the offer and its potential benefits, and (2) Prospects forget. People today forget more than ever in part because of the vast amount of data coming at them. The sales message gets fuzzier as more time passes. One simple question to ask yourself is, "Why should the prospect make the decision to buy our product or service?" The fact of the matter is, if the seller doesn't have a clear picture of the reasons to buy, how can we expect the prospect to? Sellers must learn to communicate in ways that penetrate through today's clutter.

The goal is to provide a clear, simple narrative that is compelling and memorable. But what stops sellers from messaging more clearly? The short answer: winging it. Many dynamic salespeople do a superb job of winging their sales presentation. At times, there may be no other alternative; perhaps there was little opportunity to prepare. The problem with winging it is the enormous cognitive load that it requires. Preparation plays an important role in presenting with clarity. When you're prepared, your messages are more to the point since you have thought about the points in advance.

Talking in Pictures

"A man stands on the corner with large bright-colored balloons coming out of his hat while he carries a tuba in one hand and a juicy hamburger in the other!" I actually saw this once while driving; the man was engaged in street-corner advertising for a local hamburger restaurant. Descriptive words create a scene that stir our imaginations. Whether written or spoken, these thought-provoking words resonate in people's memory and consciousness. My business partner, Peter, who is an expert at this, calls it **talking in pictures**. This involves using descriptive language to paint a picture of what doing business with you will look like. It means presenting your message in a way that takes the prospect on a mental journey focusing on the benefits of the solution.

For an example of this, consider a skilled waiter who graphically describes the menu items to a customer. Ever find yourself thinking, *Wow, everything sounds so delicious*? As the waiter is describing each dish, it seems as if he can actually taste and savor them. It's not just the words that he uses, it's his facial expressions, gestures, and tone that convey the essence of each item to the customer. Talking in pictures does not always involve the use of visual aids; however, they should be used whenever deemed appropriate.

Using Visual Aids

If a picture is worth a thousand words, visual aids are worth that and more. Visual selling tools come in many varieties: PowerPoint slides, brochures, site-sellers, flip charts, whiteboards, computer-based animations, proposal illustrations, and so on. Proper use of these tools can enhance effective presentation skills by providing timely illustrations and pictures that can impact the prospect. However, these tools can also have a negative effect if used improperly. One common misuse is depending too much on the visual aid. For example, when using PowerPoint, oftentimes people simply create slides expecting them to guide the flow of the conversation. The better practice is always to develop your presentation script first, and then create slides that support your dialogue.

Another pitfall with using visual aids comes with preparing too many slides that can bore your audience, also known as "death by PowerPoint." A best practice is to design slides that consist of no more than five bullet points, with each consisting of one to five words. The number of slides should be based on presenting each slide for about ninety to one hundred twenty seconds. This guideline ensures that your presentation is prepared for the right length of time. Moreover, whenever possible, you should include relevant graphics to drive the impact of the main themes on particular slides. Last, don't be afraid to skip slides when you need to make up time.

Omitting parts of your presentation also applies to other types of materials as well. You don't want to appear like the bad encyclopedia salesman who forges ahead with his presentation with little regard for the prospect's concerns. Salespeople are, of course, *people*, which means that the vast majority of us are also consumers. Selling is fundamentally based on treating buyers the way you'd want to be treated.

Another way to become more flexible in using visual aids is to master your content and delivery. When you know your visual aids inside and out, you are naturally more flexible and prepared to make adjustments or deal with disruptions, but just because you create the slides, and you know their content, doesn't constitute readiness to deliver. Thus, you must mentally rehearse and when possible, verbally test your delivery (dry run). In so doing, remember to allow time for questions.

In sum, visual aids should be used to assist your presentation skills and to drive the transfer of your presentation themes. The bottom line: Use the visual aids; don't allow them to use you.

Communicating Succinctly

In 2011, I joined a sales rep on a sales call at a large university in Southern California. The prospect used a competitor's product, but we were able to garner enough of their attention to evaluate our offer for their upcoming fiscal year. After several positive sales meetings, the prospect called us back and requested a follow-up presentation. The purpose of this meeting was to answer several technical questions that had come up. Our presentation started off well. The rep set the tone by recapping the last meeting and the prospect's needs. Part of our offer included software products that required integrating to the prospect's computer network. As planned, after teeing up the meeting and delivering the overview of the central theme and benefits, the rep began his presentation. He started off doing a good job of going through each aspect of the software. But as he continued, he would get off track when he came to a new menu item. Most of these menu items were not of any relevance to the customer's needs. After a while, I noticed the time starting to get away from him. Speaking for nearly an hour, he was still less than halfway through his material. Then he stumbled through a screenshot demonstration, which faltered in part because the PowerPoint images were too small to read on the projection screen. But, instead of skipping over those slides, he continued as if they were legible.

The meeting ended after two hours and forty minutes. A typical sales call of this nature should have lasted only thirty to forty-five minutes. In any event, the customer group of four was trying to hang in there because they liked our products and frankly, they really liked the sales rep. But I noticed people starting to peer at their watches just before the two-hour mark. Although the sales rep has good selling skills, his inability to present succinctly could hinder him from moving to the next level. Fortunately, this prospect ended up buying from him; but this was a near-miss situation where his error could have been fatal to the sale. Thus, we learn a valuable lesson: Be prepared, be succinct, and be clear.

The ability to convey a message succinctly is one of the most critical communication skills you can have. People tend to have a strong preference for clear, concise communication. Perhaps it's because of the enormous volume of data that fill our lives today. Whether speaking or writing, it is best to express yourself with as few words as possible. Albert Einstein once said, "Everything should be made as simple as possible, but not simpler." The goal is to communicate with clarity and within an efficient amount of time to make your case.

Drilling the Central Theme— The *Big Sexys*

In today's business communication, it seems that everything gets tagged with the *important* or *critical* label. But there's only so much the mind can handle in terms of remembering parts of a sales dialogue. Creating brilliant clarity therefore involves pulling out the sexy benefits that most impact the prospect's buying objectives. But we don't want just any old sexy benefits. We are looking for the three or four sexiest ones—the **Big Sexys**! Big Sexys represent the main ingredients of the selling offer expressed in clear, memorable phrases or talking points. You can create these themes for your customers but they tend to be more powerful when they come from them. Said another way, let the customer have the paintbrush when creating their solution masterpiece. You can shape and formulate themes based on the customer's input and this creates a stronger connection with the buyer. The following bullet points represent an actual customer's central theme. It is from the million-dollar sale to the biotech company that was discussed in Chapter 2.

Example of Big Sexys from Actual Client
(Business Equipment Industry):
- Improve client communications effectiveness
- Enhance the mail's or print center's brand perception and professionalism
- Position the mail and print center to accommodate growth trend

These themes were developed from our discovery process and were later validated by the prospect. Validation involves the buyer confirming the accuracy of the information. As a result, buyers are more engaged, which can reveal useful insights into their interest level and buying readiness.

To practice the Big Sexys is to reinforce them so they're understood throughout the selling process. You will know that you have created a compelling theme when you hear the prospect expressing it to other people. The more they hear themselves saying them, the more they sell themselves psychologically. During interactions, sellers should restate the themes often, but without sounding redundant.

In sum, identify powerful themes by using the customer's stated needs in their own words whenever possible. A noted best practice is to borrow phrases for theme starters from published information such as websites, annual reports, 10-K reports, and newsletters. Next, you want to shape the theme into a few key points that are succinct and memorable. Last, drill the central theme throughout your communication with the goal of inspiring the prospect to adopt it to their own language.

Summarizing Your Presentation

In high school and college, we learned the importance of summarizing for essays and verbal presentations. However, many sellers omit summary conclusions in their sales presentations. Summarizing is an effective tool that fosters reflection and perspective on the topic's content. An effective summary aids in driving the central themes that you want the prospects to remember and value. Any sales interaction that requires a follow-up discussion or meeting should be summarized. A conclusive summary should always be presented at the end of a sales interaction. However, you should also insert them throughout your presentation where needed. In general, the longer the presentation, the more summary checkpoints you should have. For example, during a one-hour-long presentation, you might insert three summary points at the following locations: (1) after the first topic or section is presented, (2) after the next topic or section is presented, and (3) as part of the conclusion of the presentation. The conclusive summary of every sales meeting should include next steps and any actionable items. Many times buyers do not follow through on their promised tasks because they forget. I have had buyers tell me that it's the sales rep's responsibility to prod or remind them of their tasks. Regardless, the seller must always try to do everything possible to advance the sale to the close. If that means sending a prospect a friendly reminder to perform a follow-up task, then so be it.

As salespeople, we sometimes fall into the trap of believing that every word of our presentation has equal value. Consequently, many sellers spew volumes of words at the customer in hopes that enough of them will stick. However, there are too many other things that occupy the buyer's thoughts. Therefore it's crucial that buyers understand your proposal's key points versus struggling to comprehend too many details of your presentation.

In today's world of email and social media messaging, sellers must use different mediums to send and receive sales messages. More and more buyers are using email and social media platforms as their preferred methods of sales communication. As a result, sellers must leverage other mediums (besides verbal) as needed to adapt to these changing preferences. A good rule of thumb is to take the buyer's lead on their message medium preferences. I recently had a client ask me to text him an update on his account, which was quite different than the norm. Nonetheless, after doing so, I noticed that he continued the exchange by asking questions and requesting information. The days of exclusive face-to-face selling will probably never return. Hence, today's sellers must be agile and flexible in using multiple mediums to advance their sales message. The key is to learn the customer's preferred mode of communication and their order of priority.

Written summaries involve sending written correspondence after a sales interaction to summarize the key points from the meeting. In some ways, a written theme can aid the sales process in ways that verbal messages cannot. For example, an email is portable and timeless, allowing for the recipient to read it over and over. A written message also adds a visual element to the theme, which can increase its impact and recall. You may also want to add the central theme to an email subject line or include it in the body of emails. Last, visual aids can be used to drive the theme by strengthening clarity with pictures or animation. These tools can be especially beneficial to prospects in cases where the seller is not present.

Today, with the help of technology, summaries of previous sales meetings or conferences can be included in electronic calendar invites. Salespeople also use these email systems to send the agenda for upcoming meetings. Most business email calendar systems allow you to add the follow-up meeting to the recipient's calendar. In addition, many CRMs such as Salesforce.com and others feature an integrated email system. Using a CRM email feature, messages can be sent using the customer record and historical data. Another reason these email systems can be helpful is because most of them archive all customer communications in one place. This allows you to better understand your customer's preferences as well as their reactions to certain sales messages. Summarizing through written and verbal methods helps to create a laser focus on the most important aspects of your value proposition.

As discussed in earlier chapters, this type of thin-slice messaging creates clarity for the buyer, helping him or her make the right decisions to achieve their goals.

Chapter 6

CONNECTING SKILLS AND NONVERBAL COMMUNICATION

W e have now learned that action subskills relate to the expressive aspects of PC, namely speech-related ones. Now we turn to the reaction subskills of connecting, which deal with receiving and responding to messages. Although connecting skills are implicit in nature, they can be enhanced under the right conditions.

Before we dive deeper into reaction skills, we first must understand how action activities relate to the reaction parts of connecting. In setting up favorable conditions for intuitive learning we confront the counterintuitive idea of trying to make the implicit aspects of the selling more noticeable. Note that implicit learning is acquired mostly without awareness, through routine experience. But the quality of connecting in selling is affected by the amount of cognitive demand used during the interaction. For example, a novice seller attributes most of her mental energy toward the action aspects of PC versus reaction. Her thoughts might be focused on her presentation content, making it difficult to notice implicit cues. Expert sellers, on the other hand, perform the basic action tasks with little effort, freeing their mental resources for reaction tasks.

Below are several learning activities for automating action PC skills:

1. Identify and isolate the most influential elements of your presentation content.
2. Develop these elements into a script or central talking points.
3. Identify the weakest content area and prioritize for improvement.
4. Refine and improve the skill until it can be delivered with ease.
5. Incorporate the next element and repeat the process.
6. Deliberately practice the presentation during live sales calls.
7. When possible, video record yourself, playback, and identify improvement areas.

The first three of these activities may require the assistance of a skilled coach or trusted advisor to select the right elements to work on. Through focused training action skills, your delivery becomes automatic, allowing attentional focus to be directed toward connecting.

Now, let us examine the connecting subskill of attentiveness, which relates to sustained listening and focus on the prospect message and cues.

Essential # 4: Brilliant Attentiveness

Attentiveness is a broad term that carries several meanings and interpretations. For example, a person could be described as attentive by the ability to pay attention or appear to pay attention. Others ascribe it to the level of interaction and engagement during conversations. During a sales dialogue, salespeople can become bored or disinterested, which can decrease attention and inhibit recognition. Inattention as well as attention are noticeable by the both the seller and the buyer through body language or other nonverbal cues. It's often expressed by a slight wandering of the eyes or looking down to read notes while the other person is speaking.

Conversely, eye contact, nodding, or affirmative verbal responses are signals that the buyer is connecting with your message. Thus, attentiveness is highlighted by active listening and the intent to understand. One reason salespeople struggle to listen and notice visual cues is due to noise within the sales setting. Noise plays a key role in the amount of cognitive load required to focus on action tasks. It may include talking over the prospect and focusing on counterarguments or discrediting statements. So how do you find the clear line of sight into the prospect's message? In short, *attentionality*. Recall in Chapter 3 that we discussed attentionality, which relates to an intense focus on the task at hand. We further answer this question as we discuss additional elements and strategies that enhance attentive skills.

Genuineness in Communication

We all want our communication partner to be genuine and honest. Thus, helping customers achieve their goals demonstrates genuine interest in their message. A key action to the mindset of a genuine posture is to avoid focusing on results. Instead, think of the prospect's goals and center your mind and eyes on them to learn all you can. Doing this helps to create optimal conditions for connecting. Said another way, you are more likely to actively listen to the prospect's message when you're not thinking about making the sale.

Try this imagery technique to help keep your attention on the prospect: Imagine your prospects as honest, good people who do a good job for their employer. This allows you to shape a positive perception of who they are in your mind. In addition, you should learn the personal preferences of your customers and prospects; doing so can build a stronger foundation for communication. You will likely find, as I have, that the world is a lot smaller than we sometimes think. For instance, you learn that prospects went to the same schools or have children around the same age as yours. These incidental similarities act as a bonding agent and can increase the chances of the buyer sharing more about their needs.

Showing Empathy

"What would you do if you were in my shoes?" I once had a buyer of a large government agency ask me this question. This came after he discovered that he'd made a mistake on a formal bid request that ended up excluding a competitor's ability to provide a proposal. Since my company would've been awarded the bid, my first thought was to suggest that he let the bid stand. After all, there was very little chance that the other vendors would be able to meet the bid requirements. But as I thought about it, I decided to look at the issue through the customer's eyes. It turned out that I shared his concern that purchasing standards should always be fair to all vendors. As a result of this reflection, I suggested that he reissue the bid with the corrected information.

We still earned the bid award, even though it was delayed. But I believe the decision was right, and I know that it helped strengthen our level of trust for many years thereafter. Empathy is about placing aside your personal interests and instead, mentally placing yourself in the customer's shoes. Being empathetic doesn't take a lot of work, but unfortunately it's even easier to forget its importance. It's simply making the decision that matters, and having the trust to put your customer's first.

Showing empathy toward customers and prospects is critical to becoming more attentive. Empathy shows a cooperative and respectful posture that fosters mutual cooperation. If a prospect feels or believes that the seller doesn't understand them, the seller is usually the one who suffers most. Hence, the real power of empathy goes far beyond just acting empathetic; it involves showing respect to the buyer as a person and as a professional.

I believe the vast majority of salespeople would not intentionally undermine a prospect, but many make this misstep by simply not being more aware. For instance, when dealing with an influencer level contact (aka the gatekeeper), the salesperson might come across as brash or insensitive. Managers and mentors should leverage these situations into teachable moments. During coaching interactions with salespeople, a manager could ask a reflective question such as, "What do you think this employee (gatekeeper) job entails?" Eventually, questions like these remind us to respect all employees regardless of their authority level.

A good way to practice empathy is to ask yourself, "How can I help (the gatekeeper/influencer) help me?" This allows you to ponder better ways of working with them. The better news is that your empathy will be detected by the prospect, which incites them to be more helpful to you. Empathy is essential to effective listening. It's also a critical skill that can improve your engagement with prospects. Sales empathy is putting yourself in your customer's shoes … and enjoying it.

Active Listening

According to my wife, I may be a good listener, but I could use some work on my listening skills when it comes to spousal interactions. Her case is supported by the many routine conversations like this one:

> (Wife calls me on the phone) …
> Wife: "You want to go out for dinner tonight?"
> Me: "I don't know. What do you have in mind?"

Wife: "Doesn't matter to me. What would you like to eat?"

Me: "You know that new wings place is really good. We can eat there or I can pick up a batch and bring it home. Is that OK?"

Wife: (after awkward silence) "Alright … yeah, just pick it up, and I'll see you later."

Me: "Huh? You asked me what I liked …"

Most of us can relate to this type of communication breakdown. We as people often hear what we want to hear instead of hearing the message that was intended. My wife's intention? She wanted us to go out to a nice restaurant for dinner. But instead, I heard, "What would be good to eat tonight?" and my thoughts leaped to *Wings are great tasting, especially while at home watching the game*. When you listen actively to the prospect (or your partner for that matter), you show a patient, genuine interest in their message. Through this sustained listening and tracking, your attention level to the prospect is heightened and more likely to be returned. Active listening involves listening beyond just words by seeking to truly understand the speaker's message and intentions. Consider the following important subskills of active listening:

- Making eye contact and controlling your own nonverbal cues
- Noticing the speaker's nonverbal cues: facial, tone, hands, etc.
- Avoid thinking what you will say next
- Paraphrasing the prospect's message
- Asking pertinent questions
- Summarizing the prospect's main points

Now let's explore each of these a little closer. It's important to make eye contact with your audience when you are speaking, but it's even more important with active listening. Eye contact shows the prospect that you are 100 percent focused on her message and her thoughts. It's also helpful to occasionally show the speaker that you are tracking with them as they speak. Your body language can help reflect that you are open and actively listening, such as leaning slightly forward toward the buyer. You can also use verbal affirmations to cue the buyer that you're hearing and understanding her message. Be careful here not to lose interest and merely go through the motions when you have actually been distracted. This is quickly detected by the buyer and may be interpreted as rude or insensitive.

Additional Thoughts and Ideas to Improve Attentive Skills

Reflective Listening is another attentive subskill that signals to the speaker that you are tracking with their message and ideas. One form of reflective listening is paraphrasing, where the listener restates the essence of the speaker's message to confirm understanding. It can also be used to clarify intent of the received message. When a buyer hears a paraphrase of his own words, you affirm that his message is valued and heard. This can enhance the openness of the communication. In fact, many times after hearing a paraphrase, the buyer will instinctively offer more information. When paraphrasing, be sure to avoid redundancy. You don't want to feed back every other sentence from the buyer's mouth. Try the following bridges to help transition to a paraphrase:

"So what you're saying is …"
"What you're telling me is …"
"What I heard you to mean is …"

In addition to paraphrasing, asking pertinent questions helps to improve attentive skills. In the following exchange, note how the seller uses pertinent questions that reflect listening and understanding:

Buyer: "Well, we really want to do something pretty soon because our current method is costing us too much to maintain, not to mention the loss of productivity every year trying to find parts."

Expert Seller: "I hear what you're saying. Can you tell me more about your maintenance costs? How are they affecting your daily operations and budgets?"

In this conversation, the salesperson tracks with the discussion closely by asking a logical, intuitive follow-up question. But what if the salesperson's response went like this:

Novice Seller: "OK, can you also tell me who else will be involved with the decision process?"

See the difference? Unfortunately, these types of disjointed exchanges occur far too often. Pertinent questions are relevant, well timed, and show that you are actively listening and engaged.

Summarize the Speaker's Main Points

If you have been actively listening, you'll notice the prospect smile or nod as they hear their own words played back to them. There's a feeling of, *Wow, the salesperson is listening and cares enough to make sure they've got it right.* But you'll want to make sure that you don't put words into the buyer's mouth. At times, the buyer will add, change, or clarify his message after listening to your summary. As noted previously, active listening is more than listening to the prospect's words; it's listening with your eyes as well. We now discuss nonverbal communication or **eye listening** to better understand the intent of the buyer's messages.

Nonverbal Communication: Listen with Your Eyes

Nonverbal communication relates to the perceptions of body language, facial expressions, gestures, and spatial positioning within the environment. Because these cues can be visually observed, salespeople must learn to *listen* with their eyes to gain useful customer insights. Most psychologists and communication experts estimate nonverbal elements to represent from 60 to 90 percent of overall communication. Given the dynamics of dyadic communication and the limits of research evaluation methods, the exact number may be impossible to pinpoint. But according to a 2007 study by Albert Mehrabian, empirical data reflects the breakdown of communication as follows: words (content) 7 percent, vocal elements (tone) 38 percent, and nonverbal (visual) 55 percent. If you subtract the 7 percent for words, you're left with 93 percent, but of course, 38 percent of that is the perceived tone of how someone is speaking. The exact amount of communication that is nonverbal is not as important as the fact that the vast majority of it does not involve words. Therefore, receiving nonverbal messages is an essential component of listening and relating to what the prospect is thinking and feeling. Even though you don't have to become a body language expert, improving nonverbal skills is central to developing expertise.

Negative body language is often perceived to be obvious from certain body actions. This could be a prospect folding her arms or maybe speaking with an irritable tone. But what if the conditions created a stimulus that caused someone to fold their arms, such as the temperature being very cold. Therefore, it's vital to avoid leaping to conclusions based on *single* elements of nonverbal messages. We know from practical experiences as well as through research that most people place a higher value on the tone and nonverbal elements of messages versus the words themselves. The key to effective nonverbal interpretation is noticing the ***matching*** elements between words, tone, and nonverbal cues. The idea is that when all three are supportive of each other, the message should be clear to understand. When they are out of alignment (***incongruence***), the message is unclear and difficult to interpret. Typically, people have the most control over words while tone and nonverbal signals occur subconsciously. As a result, the most common mismatch of messages involves words that don't seem to match the tone and nonverbal cues. Consider this example of incongruence messaging:

Prospect's words: "I don't see a problem with your product at all."

Prospect's tone: Sounds uncertain and concerned, voice seems flat

Prospect's nonverbal cues: Avoids eye contact, has closed posture, looks uneasy

These mismatches act as red flags that offer the seller feedback that something in the sales process may be wrong. Armed with this knowledge, you can adjust your messaging so it connects better with the prospect.

Exercise: Detecting Nonverbal Communication

You can also learn more about nonverbal cues by watching television programs with a little twist. Consider the following steps to set up this learning activity: First, find a TV show that depicts people conversing in natural settings. Ideally the dialogue should last for several minutes. Look for TV programs that involve real (nonscripted) conversations such as news interviews or panel discussions. For scripted or semi-scripted dialogues, seek out high-quality movies or TV reality shows that you have not seen. Second, you will need to have a DVR or similar device for recording the TV show. If you don't have a TV recorder, use a DVD movie with a DVD player. Third, watch a program segment or scene with two or more people talking, lasting five to ten minutes *without the sound*. Estimate what emotional and behavioral nonverbal cues the interactants convey and write down your findings. Fourth, once you have an idea of the basic intent of the message you have viewed, rewind the video and play it back *with sound*. Fifth, now compare your perceived thoughts about the message to the actual message content, looking for any variances. Repeat steps three through five as needed. You might watch the video again with and without the sound to pick up more nonverbal cues that you may have missed.

An alternative exercise is to listen to a program (sound only) but do not watch the video, then follow the same steps and notice any differences from the first exercise. With more practice, you should see improvement in your nonverbal recognition skills with customers.

Keep in mind that buyers are subconsciously and perhaps some even consciously, reading the seller's nonverbal cues at the same time. This makes it very important for you to be aware of your own nonverbal tendencies. The goal is to ensure that you are not sending unintended signals to buyers.

Spatial Nonverbal Cues

Nonverbal signals are not only conveyed through gestures, your eyes, and expressions, but they also are relayed through the use of space. Most of us have experienced that we feel uneasy when someone violates our own personal space; but the way we use space can also send more subtle messages of openness, empathy, and team spirit. For example, in a business setting, a buyer might sit across a large desk while the seller sits (facing them) on the opposite side. This is a typical seating configuration found in many offices. However, face-to-face seating tends to project a mental barrier between the two sides. In addition, presenting is more difficult when the seller has an upside-down view of her presentation materials. To remedy this, you can ask (nicely) if the prospect minds coming out from their desk and joining you at an open table (if available). If a suitable place is unavailable, you could ask if it is OK to move your chair (from sitting across from them to sitting next to them). Ideally, you want to be side by side with them but the next best location is flanked to their side. This may seem to be a minor detail, but for many salespeople, it creates a friendlier space in which to engage with your customer.

For conference room settings, a good practice is to sit in one of the side chairs closest to the chair at the front of the table. This invites the prospect to take a chair right next to you. A friendly suggestion might get them to do so but if they don't, they'll usually sit at the head end chair. Either way, this tends to decrease the probability that they will sit all the way on the opposite side of the conference table directly facing you. If you never do this, it may at first appear to be a difficult task to remember, but after following these protocols for a while, you find that your autopilot takes over. As with old bad habits, good habits are just as easy to keep, once you start them.

We have been discussing strategies to control the use of space in the environment, but can we control our own nonverbal signals? Attentionality plays a role here as well. When a salesperson is too consumed with closing the sale, her body language will convey that message. Instead, train your mind to avoid drifting to the past or future and to remain focused on the moment.

Another strategy is to ask a peer or manager to give you feedback on your negative and positive nonverbal tendencies. This allows you to recognize the cues that you want to avoid sending. For instance, you might have a tendency to lower your tone and look down when asking for the order. Many sales reps will increase their speech pace (too fast) at certain points of a dialogue. Being more aware of your nonverbal signals helps you learn to send the good ones and correct the negative ones.

Throughout life, we all have recognized nonverbal signs from others that tell us what emotions and thoughts they are feeling. In selling, these *emotional intelligence* (**EI**) skills are essential to effective PC and effect your overall performance. A heightened awareness of nonverbal cues allows you to accurately identify buyer reactions and preferences during interactions.

Another important aspect of nonverbal skill involves relating with others who share similar likes and values. While these preferences are expressed nonverbally, research methods using representative tasks allow us to see them in action with more clarity. In PBS's 2010 research documentary, *The Human Spark, Brain Matters,* an experimental research study showed that babies as early as a few months old favored the stimuli with similar preferences as their own. In one test, researchers showed a baby two plates containing food, one with green beans (purposely prepared to not be very tasteful) and the other with crackers. The toddler, like most children, chose the crackers to eat over the vegetables. The Yale University experimenter, wearing two hand puppets, performed the same test where she simulated one puppet choosing to eat the green beans and the other, the crackers. Next, the baby was given the choice of which puppet to play with; he chose the one who ate the crackers as he did. These types of studies teach us that preferences are part of our intuitive makeup as humans. With time, preferences evolve into much more subtle and subconscious behaviors. Therefore, we assume that our test-subject baby will grow up and become a corporate buyer, using his intuitive skill to make the right purchase decisions.

Microexpressions are flash instances of facial gestures that tell the true emotion or feeling of a person. Common microexpressions often involve the eyes. For instance, when we are giving our undivided attention to someone or we hear something that we like, our pupils tend to widen. As a seller, noticing a prospect's eyes could offer valuable insight into the buyer's interest level. Conversely, eyes that seem distracted and narrow could be an indicator that a buyer is not engaged or is uninterested. Fluttering eyes tend to project an underlying issue or concern. Many times, when you make eye contact with someone who does this, they will use a distraction such as rustling through papers or flipping through your proposal. Again, to avoid misinterpreting an isolated behavior, remember it is important to compare these microexpressions with words and tone. Making good eye contact with prospects can reveal useful clues about their messages. Accurately interpreting these messages enables you to send back a more tailored message that fits the prospect's goals and needs.

Mirroring

Have you ever noticed the slight change in your speech when you speak to family members or friends with different dialects? When speaking to family members from Arkansas, for example, your voice may change to more of a Southern dialect. This seems to be a natural inclination that people have, perhaps because somewhere at our deepest core values as humans, we want to be cooperative and accepted by others. Along with the desire to feel accepted, people tend to naturally gravitate toward others who share similar preferences. Mirroring, or *mimicking*, can create a more relational selling atmosphere. Reflecting the prospect's movements or language sends out positive energy that you are interested in them, their thoughts, and their words. Obviously, mirroring should be done with the utmost subtlety. Novices should first practice with a coworker, friend, or family member before trying it with their customers.

Suggestions to Improve Mirroring

There are several ways in which you can use mirroring with your customers. For instance, if you notice that a prospect runs their fingers through their hair, you might make a similar gesture during the conversation. One client of mine loved to use hand gestures when talking—his hands seemed to move with the words as he spoke. Without even realizing it, I started using hand gestures as well. Needless to say, we got along well, and he was a very loyal client for many years. A colleague who accompanied me on a sales call to this customer brought it to my attention. Another way that you can use mirroring is to borrow certain language and speech patterns from the buyer. This is a powerful technique that works wonders. People love to hear their own words fed back to them. Mirroring gives us a feeling of being understood when others relate to our thoughts, ideas, and preferences. It can also make us more persuasive. Let's say a prospect tends to use an affirmative phrase such as, "OK, you with me?" throughout their speech. You could mirror this by inserting a similar phrase like, "Right, you with me?" If the phrase is too unique, it may not be a good idea to repeat it verbatim unless you have a very strong trust level.

Ed Diba liked to repeat his customer's acronyms, which was a very successful mirroring technique. It seems that virtually every industry in the business culture uses acronyms as part of their daily language. It is one of the distinguishing factors that almost anyone can spot when company employees are talking. Professional salespeople want to be seen as insiders through the eyes of their customers. Sharing the same acronym vocabulary can make a difference in your ability to connect. Just make sure you know what the acronym stands for before using it. Now, let's take a look at this list of nonverbal gestures and actions used for mirroring:

Hands	Body Movements	Vocal Tone
Touching or rubbing hair, face, neck, opposite shoulder	Leaning back or forward in chair	Inflection, pitch, phrase patterns, volume
Hand resting on face or neck or arms, raised finger	Tilting head Leaning forward	Speech pacing
Talking while using hand gestures	Standing posture— hands on hips, arms folded	Speech patterns
"Steepling" (fingertips together) Fingers locked (but not clinched)	Sighing (but avoid negative sighs)	Style, formalities, informalities, dialect

Mirroring Traps and Behaviors to Avoid

I once had a sales team member—Jackie—who was very much into politics. His car was decorated with all kinds of political bumper stickers, and he couldn't go very long in a conversation without asserting his political views. One day during a ride-along, Jackie began bringing up political issues to customers. He was very opinionated and criticized the opposing party's candidates. The problem was that he had no idea what particular political preference his customer may or may not have had. As a result, he may have jeopardized sales opportunities on the basis of criticizing someone's political preferences. Moreover, even if the customer supported the same party or had no preference, they may have still been turned off by his type of behavior. As salespeople, we want to connect with prospects on lighter, less sensitive areas so as to ensure high professional standards.

I believe that Jackie thought he was simply engaging in harmless small talk that he felt his customers would identify with. But in reality, he was also taking a huge risk given the explosive nature of politics. My belief is that salespeople should keep it in neutral when dealing with potential controversial or sensitive subjects. But to be clear, mirroring a prospect does not suggest trying to become someone you're not.

The fact that most communication is nonverbal indicates that people naturally send these messages subconsciously. But can mirroring be performed consciously and intentionally? The answer is yes, but with caution. While mirroring can be an effective method to persuade buyers, intentional mirroring, if overused, could backfire due to excessive cognitive strain. If this happens, unwanted nonverbal signals may result. My suggestion is to use the mirroring material from this book and other sources to heighten your awareness, then gradually work mirroring into your routine. Also, remember to think with empathy toward your customer while actively listening.

Consider this rhetorical question: How many chances do you get to make a good first impression? Part of the salesperson's core job duties is to interact with many types of people and personalities. For example, the reason salespeople don't usually wear loud-colored suits or flamboyant jewelry is because they could create a negative perception for some buyers. A negative first impression is hard to overcome, so why create one in the first place? The same goes with displaying personal preferences that could create a wall between you and your customer.

Mirroring should be done while focusing your attention solely on the prospect. This allows you to naturally adapt your style to that of your customer. To borrow another analogy from my colleague Mike Christie, "Adapting is like the chameleon—when salespeople interact with prospects, they adapt on the outside, to blend in with their clients, increasing the odds for success." Like the chameleon, the seller does not change who they really are on the inside. This analogy always brings a smile to my face because I think of my good friend Mike. Not only is he one of the best sales trainers I know, he's also one of the funniest people I've ever met. Mike's expertise, like other sales experts, is largely due to his ability to put people at ease and relax. We now turn our attention to the easiest of all communication skills: the smile.

Smile . . . It's Contagious

Nothing seems more universal to all humans than the joy of laughter or a simple smile. It is one of the oldest and most effective ways to quickly change a person's attitude. Whether it be emotions such as sadness, anger, uptightness, or just plain old mundaneness, a smile always seems to help. Years ago, as a new sales rep, I was on a ride-along with my trusted coach and training manager, Mark Giganti. After making a few calls, Mark informed me that my sales approach was good, but he added I was missing one thing: a smile! Mark explained that he could see the prospect's facial expressions respond much like mine (which were very serious and businesslike). I figured, here's a guy that had literally taught me and a bunch of other green new hires to operate and professionally demonstrate the most sophisticated paper-handling machines in the company in a matter of a few days. What did I have to lose? So I tried it, and sure enough, the first prospect I greeted with a big smile sent one back to me. This seemed to foster a more upbeat, interactive exchange. From that day forward, I've been striking a genuine smile whenever I greet a prospect face to face.

How powerful is a smile? During one of my training seminars, a student asked this question of an expert seller: "How do you deal with getting kicked out of a business when you're cold calling?" The expert replied, "I have never been thrown out! Sure, there may have been a few prospects who seemed a bit perturbed over my unannounced visit, but my smile tames them long enough for a short, professional exchange. I just kill 'em with kindness!"

It's also good to insert smiles during the sales dialogue. Heck, it may even help to smile as you write your sales emails, tweets, or social media messages; it certainly can't hurt! I'm not talking about fake smiling like we often do when someone suddenly wants to snap our picture. Research shows that these fake smiles can be detected by the lack of facial muscle movement around the mouth and eyes. Known as the "Duchenne smile," genuine smiles of pleasure and happiness involve muscle engagement around the eyes and mouth areas. Therefore, make sure your smiles are real and learn to notice the genuine or fake smiles from prospects.

A smile conveys a positive communication posture, and it can help you relax, which in turn relaxes the prospect. At times, this relaxation can go further where smiles can turn into laughter or light humor, but be careful to exercise good old common sense in this area.

In business, we use humor in selective ways to better relate and connect with prospects. The best humor tends to include more spontaneity and has good timing. Bad humor has the opposite effect; it comes across as predictable and feels awkward and at the wrong time or place. Humor is not the same as telling jokes. Jokes are risky in a professional setting and often miss the mark. In addition, many professionals consider jokes in a public setting, outside of friends or family, to be inappropriate. Smiling and a little light humor can be useful in building rapport and shaping a more favorable perception of who you are to your customers. So the next time you're facing that moment of truth, about to make your sales approach, don't think of getting rejected, just flash those pearly whites and kill 'em with a little kindness (smile).

How can you leverage nonverbal skills to improve intuitive ability and sales performance? The good news is that these skills can be learned and grown into intuitive expertise over time. Your ability to recognize nonverbal cues represents a window of the expert seller's advantage. Sending positive nonverbal signals such as smiling and mirroring also help to boost intuitive skill. Given that these perceptual abilities are activated all the time, improving them should be practiced daily. In addition, using video from a webcam or smartphone can be an excellent self-practice tool for capturing your nonverbal expressions. In section three, we will discuss more of these self-training actions in greater detail. First though, we continue our journey by exploring sales connecting skills and how to acquire them more quickly.

Chapter 7

PERCEPTIVENESS AND RESPONSIVENESS SKILLS

Essential #5: Brilliant Perceptiveness

The following story derives from conversations with "Pat," a sales team member, after our interactions with a customer in the medical equipment industry. Given Pat's impressive selling expertise, I decided to probe his thinking after each sales call we made together in order to gain insights on why he reacted in certain ways. On the initial visit with the customer, Pat prequalified them for one of our advanced software products. The customer was receptive to our offer and responded by setting up a follow-up meeting. During the second visit, Pat inquired about integrating our software with the company's order management system (OMS). Gary, the principal decision maker, told us that he had problems dealing with his OMS vendor, which he viewed as unreasonable. He stated in no uncertain terms that he preferred not to deal them any further. As Gary continued, Pat noticed that his body language conveyed concern, like a feeling of being unsettled about something. His facial expressions came across as nervously optimistic. Upon further questioning, Gary admitted that his OMS was becoming obsolete but the vendor was asking forty-five thousand dollars for upgrades. As a result, Gary felt he was being pressured to upgrade to the new system at an inflated price.

The next day, my team met to figure out the best way to provide the solution to meet the customer's needs. Our technical specialist made it clear that we would need to connect our software to the OMS in order to meet this goal.

Pat and I met with Gary and his operations manager for a third meeting. Immediately, he could see the customer was concerned about making any changes to his OMS. Gary brought it up again, recalling the negative experience with his OMS vendor. As he spoke, Pat noticed that when he began to explain the OMS issue, his body language and tone appeared similar to that of other clients he had experienced. Gary's voice shifted to a more concerning tone as he described the problem. He shook his head as he gestured toward a nearby computer screen—one of the OMS workstations. The tone and language Gary used fit the same pattern as our previous discussion, so Pat decided to change course and address the concern. At that moment, Pat recalled previous scenarios where his customers had overcome similar issues. I noticed Pat began connecting with Gary, looking him in the eye and showing empathy. Gary started to listen. At this point, Pat informed him that we would not subject him to having to make major changes to his OMS. After hearing about clients that Pat had helped to overcome similar issues, Gary grew more relaxed and engaging. Here is a summary of Pat's response:

- He aligned his goal with Gary's and made sure he knew that his concerns were understood.
- He presented two alternative methods that would avoid or minimize the OMS issue.
- He painted a hypothetical picture using the alternative methods. This created a new vision of how our solution could add value and solve Gary's concerns.
- He skipped the technical questionnaire part of his presentation. This avoided highlighting Gary's negative association with his OMS vendor. Instead, Pat saved it for a more opportune time where he could condition the discussion. His Spidey-sense was telling him that going through that questionnaire at that moment could have been a deal breaker. Pat's decision to share insights from other customers disrupted Gary's thinking and neutralized the OMS problem. Notably, this allowed him to continue through the sales process.

This entire sequence occurred within the first few minutes of the meeting. The conversation gained momentum and flowed smoothly into a very productive discussion.

Upon leaving the meeting, I peppered Pat with questions. I wanted him to become aware of his own thinking that turned the situation and to keep the sale moving. At first, he didn't understand why I was so interested. After all, he hadn't received the sales order yet and frankly, as one of the top reps in the company, he had closed much larger deals. Out of his own curiosity, he decided to ask me questions about what I observed. I told him that because of the customer's initial tone, the sale could have easily gone south but for his intuitive response. Finally, I mentioned that since our product price would cost at least twice that of the OMS upgrades, most reps would have given the sale only a small chance of closing. This exchange prompted me to reflect on the details of Pat's interaction, which led me to document several of his intuitive actions. It is from Pat's willingness to allow me to learn from him that makes it possible for me to articulate this story.

After reflecting on the calls with Gary, and speaking in depth with Pat, his actions can be described as *adaptive* selling. He adjusted his sales message by listening intently to Gary's concerns before offering new insights that changed his thinking. Said another way, it was a matter of detecting cues, quickly figuring out what they meant, and reacting to his concerns. With respect to the OMS obstacle, when we sat down with Gary, we discovered an export feature in the OMS that allowed us to accomplish the task. Within a couple of weeks, Gary placed a new sales order with Pat, and he remains a delighted customer.

My goal in this chapter is to answer the salesperson's simple question, "What can I do to truly understand my customer's communication?" To answer, we discuss perceptual skills and how we use them to form meaning and insights for customers. During sales interactions, expert sellers perform PC as follows:

1. Actively listening while monitoring nonverbal buying cues
2. Discovering the prospect's buying needs and objectives within the situation context
3. Developing prospect insights
4. Generating and presenting multiple solution options
5. Evaluating presentation effectiveness
6. Continuing to monitor the dialogue for useful cues and feedback

Sales messages can have a myriad of different interpretations with buyers, but through active listening and connecting, we convey and understand messages better. In a typical selling dialogue, the speed at which messages are constructed, evaluated, and responded to is truly a human phenomenon. In fact, language, to a certain extent, remains a mystery to science. We can form eloquent language at the speed of thought without preplanning what we want to say. Therefore, our goal is to break down these perceptual actions by describing them in sort of a slow-motion way. This helps to illuminate the underlying elements of perceptual expertise. The idea is to advance perceptual skills more rapidly by unraveling the mental actions that are at work. The learning goal is to locate *where* the expert perceptual advantage is versus trying to figure out how to do it.

By understanding perceptual actions, we heighten our awareness and create the conditions for improvement. For instance, this is likened to shopping for a new car, and afterward, spotting more cars like the one you test drove or purchased. Psychologists refer to this phenomenon as ***observational selection bias***. The bigger takeaway is the fact that anyone can walk into a car dealership tomorrow and the same thing would occur. Hence, when we become aware of our perceptual actions, we create the conditions to be more perceptive. Said more simply, you can see more of what others do not when you decide you want to see it.

Interpreting the Conversational Goals of Your Prospect

Perceptual skill involves understanding the prospect's goals within the context of each selling interaction. Is the prospect in a learning mode whereby they are seeking information on a perceived problem or issue? Perhaps they have already moved past the learning stage and are now evaluating which vendor can best address their needs. Developing a perceptive understanding of your overall sales vision is largely based on the goals of the prospect. Perceptual skills help you to sniff out these goals in real time during PC. The use of responsive questions can be used to further validate and clarify customer intentions. When you know what your customer wants to achieve, you can better shape the conversation into what they expect. Conversely, if you find that their goals lack the right tactics, you can offer new insights to reset them to achieve what they really want.

So how do perceptual skills actually work? Well, outside of *magic,* the best way to understand them lies in what psychologists call **pattern recognition**. This is a cognitive process that involves noticing communication regularities and comparing them to other patterns stored in memory.

As I describe it with these words, it may seem like a lot to absorb but remember, as salespeople, we use perceptual skills on a regular basis. For instance, think of the last time you received a *no* or adverse decision from a prospect. Before hearing the explicit words, you probably sensed there was some bad news coming. It was the prospect's body language, tone, and expression that tipped you off. Likewise, pattern recognition occurs when you receive a *yes* response. There is a sense of the affirmative decision, before actually hearing the verbal *yes.* Communication patterns exist throughout the selling interaction. When you notice these cues as they occur, the patterns become clearer each time.

Drawing Meaning from Messages

It is beyond the scope of this book to expand on the many complexities of the brain or the functional depth of the RPD model, but the following is a simplified construct of pattern recognition in perceptual selling skills:

1. As information flows in through the selling environment, the brain detects potentially useful messages.
2. The cognitive processes compare the recognized message with related knowledge to determine whether a situation is known or not.
3a. If the situation is known, choices may be accessed from a memory bank of solutions and presented to the prospect.

3b. If the situation is an unknown, a different cognitive action is taken that tests potential solutions from similar situations or from creative, spontaneous ideas. The test is to decide whether to generate a particular solution or not. This cognitive process goes on until a solution is produced that best addresses the situation.

It should be noted that this description took me several minutes to write but the brain can go through this type of evaluation in milliseconds. If you blink once as fast as you can, that's one hundred fifty milliseconds! So what's the takeaway from all of this brain talk? You can learn to sell more perceptively by peeling back your mental actions to discover how you were thinking during a particular selling sequence, similar to the football player who learns from watching video by recreating his thinking during the tasked situation (football play).

Thin-Slicing: Perceptual Speed and Accuracy

Recall the case story earlier in this chapter involving Gary at the medical equipment company. As I related, within a few minutes of the discussion, Pat made a snap judgment on changing the course of the conversation. This judgment occurred in real time, which allowed him to respond appropriately to the customer. Research suggests that thin-slicing in communication, even when observing a few seconds, is very accurate when compared to assessing an entire interaction. Thin-slicing is therefore a subskill of perceptiveness. It can be hastened not by explicit training but with implicit learning and intentional experiences.

We have already noted that the speed of accessing tacit and situational knowledge represents a key difference between experts and other performers. Studies reveal that journeymen often have the same routine knowledge as experts. As Fadde asserts, experts can access the right knowledge faster and more accurately and therefore speed becomes an operational representation of cognitive load. Recall from the intro the analogy of the musical scales. The expert musician is able to apply the scale knowledge to play complex musical performances with a high degree of skill. She plays the music brilliantly by applying the scale patterns more quickly and with less cognitive effort than the novice. In selling, this bedrock principle applies to a tee. Aspiring sales experts can reduce their perceptual learning curve by reflecting on patterns during routine selling.

Another influential factor of interpreting messages is knowing the particular situation and context from which the information comes. In Chapter 2, we discussed situation selling and the most common scenarios. We now draw from that discussion to examine how perceptual skills function, in part, by accessing situation knowledge. Let's say that a prospect requests to see references of other users of your product before making their decision to buy. Based on your experience, this may suggest an underlying concern, perhaps, with your product's reliability. But what if the situation were that the customer making this request had a recent bad experience with a similar product from another vendor? The interpretation of this request would likely be different as a result of the context. Reflecting on customer situations allows you to use relevant knowledge faster, thereby boosting perceptual skills.

Discovering Insights

Now that you have interpreted the prospect's message, how do you mentally synthesize it to make sure it is applied in the best possible way? By creating *insights*. As communication is received and matched with knowledge, new ideas and approaches emerge. These ideas are often referred to as customer insights. Insights can be defined as undiscovered information provided to the buyer by the seller that creates value. A litmus test for an insight is to compare the discovered information to what the customer knows or believes. If the information can help the customer achieve their goals, and they are unaware of it, it could be an insight. Insights are used to create compelling events that encourage buyers to act. However, B2B buyers may be required to make changes to their business processes in order to benefit from insights. The question then arises, "How do you leverage insights into a compelling message for prospects?" We now prepare to talk through the final element of connecting, which deals with conveying the right message needed to achieve your selling objective.

Essential #6: Brilliant Responsiveness

A Thought Experiment

Imagine with me, if you will, this scenario: You are a decision maker for a large commercial real estate company, and you've learned that all of the pipes in one of your buildings have to be replaced. A compliance agency has informed you that better piping is needed to meet new standards and requirements. The agency has also provided you with a list of vendors that offer tubing products. After doing some research online, you narrow your search down to two vendors. You've invited each vendor to your office to discuss their products.

The first company (Apex Tubing), is actually the current vendor that installed the pipes in your building years ago. Apex sends out the account rep, "Alex," to discuss your needs. During the initial meeting with Alex, you explain receiving the compliance notice. You further discuss that you're seeking to learn about your options to install new tubing. Alex responds as follows:

(After the pleasantries): "Yes, I have been in here several times over the last year trying to warn your company about compliance. I couldn't get anywhere, just pushed off to purchasing and they said I'd have to wait until an RFP was created. But anyway, now you are going to have to do something. I can help you figure out the best tubing so you don't end up getting wacked with those compliance fines. I've seen where they can get pretty expensive, especially if you wait too long to invest. But I can show you ways to replace your tubing at a good price compared to the price of compliance fines. Now let me ask you some questions regarding your building that need to become compliant …"

Now fast forward to the next vendor meeting. This one is with BH Metals and their sales rep, "Sam." After going through a similar explanation of the situation, you listen to Sam's response:

(After the pleasantries): "Although I realized you contacted us due to the compliance issue you're facing, it's actually a great opportunity for us to take a look at all of your buildings' overall tubing to ensure you have safe, cost-efficient, and long-term reliability in them. We can go through the assessment and still meet your compliance deadlines, that way you can be more proactive and understand your overall facility needs and situation. This allows you to better manage your maintenance, repairs, and replacement costs more effectively. How does that sound to you?"

These are two very different sales responses. Alex decides to try to leverage the compliance issue as the basis of the sale. The problem with this approach is that it tends to come across as a pressure tactic. This is not to say that in some cases this approach can't work; but when you get right down to it, who really wants to be told that they *have* to buy something? As consumers, it is usually a much better feeling to *want* to buy. Sam realizes this by minimizing the compliance issue and centering his attention on the prospect's *overall* needs. Perhaps Sam's knowledge bank accessed situations of previous prospects who were turned off when made to feel that they *had* to buy. Through connecting, Sam creates a sales message that is more likely to receive a favorable response. Notice Sam's response includes the potential for new insights of evaluating *all* buildings for better overall cost management. These insights could strike a chord with the buyer as well as separate his company from other vendors.

After interpreting cues from prospect messages, we arrive at the final stage of connecting: *responsiveness*. Within PC, responsive skills center on finding the appropriate message and delivering it at the most opportune time. There are several critical success factors involved with responsive skills, namely:

- *Predicting* the prospect's readiness and need for the pending sales message,
- *Creating the right message* that achieves both the prospect's and the sales goals,
- Determining *the right message timing*, and
- *Delivering the message* effectively.

We have all heard the saying, "We both really just clicked," or "She and I hit it off the first time we talked." These reflect the predictive elements of PC. The idea is to communicate what the buyer wants to hear while sensing the response. As the process repeats, *message flow* occurs. Message flow is marked by a fluid dialogue with minimal effort. This can be both good and bad for salespeople. It's good because of the strong sense of connection with the buyer, which fosters more openness. An open dialogue is always welcomed because it's a lot better than the alternative of rejection.

The downside of message flow occurs when the seller is lulled into assuming that dialogue equates to buyer's readiness and ability to buy. But some buyers simply enjoy chatting. Perhaps there's a genuine rapport, but it doesn't always mean they want to do business. The key to avoiding this type of trap is to ensure that you are engaged in PC versus general communication. With PC, you guide the conversation toward the sales goals that satisfy the buyer's and seller's interests. Of course, PC also includes rapport building and learning the prospect's preferences; but achieving the sales goal is the essence of PC and therefore should be the standard by which to claim success. In sum, mental predicting within PC is part of an intuitive response mechanism that best positions your sales message. This dialogue is reflective of the level of interest in both the buyer's and seller's messages.

Most salespeople can attest to the fact that some conversations flow well, while others seem awkward and out of sync. Message adapting is a key selling action within PC that fosters better dialogue flow and momentum. Effective sales messages depend on alignment with the buyer's goals as well their anticipated thoughts and beliefs.

In some cases, sellers actually learn a lot about the buyer's needs and goals. Unfortunately, this information is not always used. A common example of this occurs when the salesperson performs a "needs analysis" survey. Once the information is collected from the buyer, the seller analyzes it. At this point, he typically directs his attention to generating the solution proposal with minimal or no buyer involvement. When the buyer finally receives the sales proposal, it can seem too canned and detached from their original intent. This naturally leads to hesitations or objections that can put the sale at risk. Thus, experts generate effective sales messages that *feel* personalized and relevant to the decision maker.

What is it that guides sellers to know the most opportune time to deliver a particular message to the prospect? The answer lies within the collection of cues received from the prospect. We can begin to answer this question by first focusing on when *not* to present certain messages. Message timing is an important component of connecting. Determining the right moment to present relates not only to the day of the sales interaction, but also to the timing within each dialogue.

A common scenario where sellers err is providing product information to meet an explicit need. Sellers tend to get very excited when they find that they have qualified the prospect for their product. This excitement often leads to talking about it. By putting the cart before the horse, PC can quickly be derailed when prospects persist in discussing the product in depth before being qualified.

Conversely, many sellers wait too long to deliver their sales message. This can occur when trying to avoid prematurely communicating the sales solution, but in doing so, missing the ideal time to share it. In reality, decision makers continue through the buying cycle internally even when salespeople are not involved. Many times, in these cases, buyers make false assumptions about the product, which may be hard to undo.

How do salespeople decide the most opportune time to respond to messages? Is it the Spidey-sense that tells you not now, wait for later, or seize the immediate moment during a discussion? Much like a skilled standup comedian timing his punchline, connecting skills guide you to the information you'll need to decide the right time to present. In addition, factoring in the overall goals and the situation helps time your message for maximum impact. During PC, the optimal moment of message timing is based on achieving the most impact while maintaining message flow.

At times salespeople may delay sharing certain messages because of the potential of being adversely perceived by the buyer. This can backfire when buyers learn of the information too late. Keep in mind, buyers also use Spidey-sense to detect when sellers withhold sales information, especially if it's perceived to be adverse to the seller. Appropriate disclosure messages should therefore be shared as early as possible to avoid breakdowns. Through sales connecting, sellers improve responsive skills by presenting the right message for the right situation at the right time.

Once the timing of the message is cognitively vetted, it is delivered to the prospect. Notably, I've been describing responsive actions by slowing down the thought process for learning purposes. But keep in mind, these cognitive actions actually occur with great speed and fluidity. Once messages are expressed with words and nonverbal signals, they move to the action stage of PC. Recall in Chapter 5 we discussed the action essentials that are used to enhance message clarity and effectiveness. As messages are exchanged, the connecting process recycles as the seller monitors the reactions of the prospect to best position his next sales message.

Adaptive Responses in PC

Adaptive responses are determined by the seller's level of product knowledge, industry knowledge, and experience in understanding customer issues. Delivering an effective response relies on the convergence of PC and adaptive skills. An adaptive response does *not* mean simply adhering to whatever suggestion the prospect wants, but rather it involves presenting insights that you believe will advance the prospect's goals. We turn now to explore adaptive selling opportunities that regularly occur in sales.

Adaptive Response to Communication Style or Preferences

During PC, it's important to notice the prospect's messaging patterns and tendencies. Does she speak in a faster or slower pace? Does she have a noticeable accent or dialect? What type of overall tone does she project? Answers to these and other style questions will help in discovering useful cues and insights for sales adapting. Once you determine the prospect's style or preferences, the conditions are set to adjust her own style to match. Like nonverbal mirroring, aspects of verbal messages can also be mimicked. Expert performers apply these verbal adapting skills to better connect with prospects. Examples of verbal adapting could range from repeating "yeah" versus "yes," "you guys" versus "y'all" to speaking with similar dialects and phrases used by the prospect. As you read these phrases, note that the best way to learn from verbal mimicking is through audio and video examples.

Adaptive Response to Business Culture and Industry Protocols

Another way to use adaptive responses is by mimicking the prospect's business culture and industry language. From time to time, salespeople use improper industry terms during the sales process. For instance, when selling to a nonprofit organization, many sales reps mistakenly say, "Your profits will increase." A misstep like this could hinder connecting with the buyer. (Nonprofits generally do not use the term *profits*; they may define revenue that is left over after expenses and taxes as *surplus* or *gains).* Effective sales messages should therefore adapt to the prospect's business culture and industry jargon. The following example highlights the use of business and industry language adapting:

Dialogue Setting—A medical software sales rep approaches a hospital prospect. Notice the differences in the *good-to-best* dialogue samples.

Sales Rep (Good—Novice): "We recently came out with a new system for hospitals that takes care of all of your compliance requirements. It also saves time and money on your billings using our automatic mailing address feature."

Sales Rep (Better—Journeyman): "I've been working with several health care organizations and showing them our new HIPAA (Health Insurance Portability and Accountability Act) compliant CRM. It does many things to help your business such as improve your billings, compliance, accounting, and everything to do with your patient data."

Sales Rep (Best—Expert): "I've been working with several clients within the health care community on our new patient processing solution. One of them reported that patient liability risks are under control using our HIPPA compliant solution, while the RCM (revenue cycle management) was cut by 40 percent. This has resulted in a net cash flow improvement of over 30 percent."

The expert's *initial benefit statement* (**IBS**) version may appear to be much longer, but in fact conveys more clarity when spoken. The extra phrasing is mainly used for industry terms that connect to the buyer's language. The novice's approach contains generalities and does not leverage the hospital's lingo. Despite the better journeyman's IBS using the specific compliance language, it still falls short because it offers too many items to think about while lacking specific benefits.

Adaptive Response to the Buying Process

In Chapter 2, we looked at a table that contrasted the typical sales process with the buying process (Table 2.2). Often, these cycles can fall out of alignment, which creates a suboptimal atmosphere for success. We now expand a bit on the buying process as related to the rise of insight selling.

Recently, I read an article entitled "The End of Solution Sales." The article suggests that solution selling is soon to be obsolete due to the proliferation of online data accessible to buyers. Central to the author's argument is the idea that buyers have less dependency on sellers, especially during the earlier buying stages. Buyer's ability to access more sales material online is ascribed as the main reason for the new trends. This mainly applies in very large sales enterprises or niche industries. However, it is relevant to all selling organizations to the extent that customers today are more informed than ever before they engage salespeople. As a result, we must change the buyer's view of the situation in cases where it is flawed or lacking information (insights).

In the B2B space, the type of organization can dictate certain buying procedures that drive the sales methods used. For instance, many territories may include commercial and government accounts. Government agencies tend to have a very different buying process than that of a commercial business. Differences range from how budgets and funding work to the procedures and requirements of purchasing decisions. In many sales organizations, sellers can expand territory opportunity and increase sales by improving their selling ability to more types of prospects. Using government selling as an example, the sales process normally begins with the contracts department, which is typically responsible for administering the purchasing procedures and budget. With commercial selling, the sale most often starts with a key stakeholder within the functional area where the product will be used.

We have now worked our way through the intuitive connecting process as a way to better understand these underlying cognitive actions.

As we close our discussion on connecting, one important timing question remains: "Should connecting be applied throughout the entire PC interaction or just during selected parts of it?"

It is recommended to always be ready to notice key information from buyers. But there are several common scenarios where buyers tend are or more apt to share useful information. You should exercise a high-alert state of readiness during the following situations:

1. Within the first few minutes of the selling interaction
2. Immediately following a salesperson's question regarding a buyer's agreement or commitment to any of the following:
   • Match needs to a product or service (qualify)
   • Advance the sales process to the next stage
   • Make a buying decision on a proposed price, terms, and conditions

Buyers will often disclose their needs and how they perceive them to be served early in the engagement. These early conversations represent an ideal time for connecting. Many times buyers convey their needs in vague terms, especially earlier in the sales process. Sellers must be able to connect in order to pull out the true meaning of these implicit messages.

During these early stages, it is important for the seller to monitor the interest level and responses of the prospect. In situations where there is low interest, the seller may have to continue building value before moving to the next step. One way to gauge a prospect's interest level is to suggest they perform a simple follow-up task. For example, a manufacturer's sales rep might ask the prospect to provide samples for testing on a proposed product. Or a transportation broker rep might request a freight cost report to analyze for possible cost savings. If the prospect agrees to perform the request, this could indicate a suitable interest level in your product. A negative or no response could suggest a lack of interest, which helps in deciding your response.

Selling today involves mutually agreeable decisions and commitments by both sellers and buyers. When salespeople pose direct questions aimed at advancing the sales process, prospects tend to reveal more of their thoughts and interests. Generally speaking, the further along in the sales cycle, the more likely prospects will communicate their true intentions and thoughts. Hence, pricing and terms negotiations represent high-alert situations for connecting.

In sum, the effortless performance of PC action skills is a prerequisite for building expertise. Applying minimal effort for action tasks frees cognitive resources to be used for reaction (connecting). Over time, with practice, connecting skills also become automatic and subconscious, thereby advancing intuitive expertise.

Summary and Reflections on Section Two

- The PC *action* essentials (planning, pausing-silence, and clarity) represent the behavioral skills required for effectively executing PC. Action skills must be mastered in order to free cognitive focus for reaction tasks.
- The PC *reaction* essentials *Connecting* (attentiveness, perceptiveness, and responsiveness) depict the implicit recognition skills most responsible for selling expertise.

- The improvement to selling expertise is hastened through the mastery of the essential PC skills—becoming brilliant at the basics.

SECTION 3

ACCELERATING THE DEVELOPMENT OF SELLING EXPERTISE

Chapter 8

PERFORMANCE-
BASED LEARNING
HASTENING SKILLS
THROUGH ROUTINE WORK

F or many years, professionals have sought ways of speeding up skill development. Organizations use on-the-job training activities such as mentoring and executive coaching to develop people while reducing training costs; but results for these activities can vary greatly depending on many factors. In the B2B arena, salespeople work mostly alone, making it hard to spend quality time learning from experts. There are favorable conditions however in the retail space, where the top expert sellers often work in close proximity. But in either B2B or B2C, the amount of time given to learn from peers is minimal. As a result, in this chapter, we will introduce creative learning activities uniquely aimed at improving skills through routine work.

Expertise is not something you can learn in a single course or classroom event. It's often related to years of practice and experience. In fact, many have asked the question, "How long does it take to become an expert?" Researchers such as Ericsson and Dr. Gary Klein estimate that it takes about ten thousand hours of practice and experience to reach expert-level performance. This works out to about twenty hours of deliberate practice per week over ten years. Keep in mind, this level reflects the highest world-class standard. Salespeople typically work a minimum of forty hours per week. As noted earlier, large amounts of deliberate practice are impractical for business people due to their schedule demands.

So when do salespeople actually practice? The answer varies. Some are fortunate to receive well-designed training with ample practice time, which helps to transfer skills to the job. Others miss the mark by having to endure heavy lecture formats that discourage retention. Many of these courses attempt to train too many skills while failing to allow enough time for practice. The vast majority of sales training is predominantly skill-execution based. As we have discussed, advanced sellers rely on cognitive-based implicit skills to move to the expert level.

That said, deliberate practice should be used whenever possible. Also, there are some training firms that offer skill courses that include 75 percent practice. A few of these firms can also provide services on how to increase or add practice into existing training curriculum. While deliberate practice can complement training by driving skill transfer to the job, it plays a much smaller role in overall selling expertise.

In addition, researchers offer several theories to drive expertise in business and other naturalistic domains. In recent years, Dr. Fadde, Dr. Klein et.al have explored the question of how to speed up expertise in natural settings. We draw from this research to present Performance-Based Leaning® (PBL) activities, designed to improve skills faster during routine work. PBL activities are modeled from Klein and Fadde's Action Learning Activities' (ALAs) deliberate performance framework:

estimating, experimenting, explaining, extrapolating, examining, exchanging, and expert coaching (Fadde and Klein, 2010).

Experience left to its own natural course can take many more years to develop than is necessary. As such, the implicit learning curve is much longer without PBL. A good analogy for PBL is likened to the GPS in the example described in the preface (driving from New York to Los Angeles). The trip is made faster and more efficient with a GPS. Thus, PBL speeds the journey to selling expertise, in part, by reframing the intent of routine work to learning.

Attentionality as a Foundation for PBL

What were you thinking when you made your last sales call? Can you recall your thoughts just before you walked into the customer's office or as the consumer entered your showroom? Think closely and recall if any of these responses fit your mindset:

- "I have to close this deal today. This looks like a great opportunity."
- "Let's see. I have to go through my questionnaire so I can figure out what I can sell him."
- "This guy's not going to buy anything. He's probably just looking."
- "First I'm going to go over his questions, then I will present my proposal and pricing."
- "Darn, I was supposed to send Jerry that email. Maybe I can get back to him tomorrow instead …"

These are all typical results-oriented thoughts that occur subconsciously as we go about our work. By changing our attentionality, our thoughts are redirected from past or future distractions to the present task at hand. To put it simply, your mind is focused on your purpose, in the present moment and without prejudice.

Consider the difference in the mindset of the attentional-focused seller:

- "Listen closely to the prospect's perspective and be sure to follow up on signals that help or halt the sales process."
- "When I deliver my benefit summary, watch the prospect's reaction to see his interest and approval level."
- "After I present a buying advantage, make sure I allow prospect to absorb and reflect."
- "Be ready for a 'risk objection' since her concern seems to be changing their procedures to fit the automation changes."
- "Be mindful with language when discussing their current process because the Ops Manager will be in the meeting and could take offense."

In sum, by reframing your focus, intuitive decision making and awareness is heightened.

Performance-Based Learning® Activities

PBL works by enabling salespeople to optimize tacit knowledge through daily work experiences and observations. It is designed to speed up skill growth and performance by fusing a convergence of learning and work. We begin our discussion of PBL by describing each activity as follows:

List of PBL Activities

- Task "Predicting"
- Task "Piloting"
- "Call" Reflection

- "Storyboarding"
- Task "Modeling"
- Expert Coaching

Predicting (estimating) aims to increase implicit knowledge by predicting responses and outcomes of targeted tasks and comparing the predictions to the actual result.

Piloting (experimenting) is designed to increase the impact of a successful task or method by attempting new ways to improve upon it.

Reflection (extrapolating) involves reflective learning through experiences. Sellers apply cause-and-effect thinking analysis to develop lessons learned for future sales calls.

Storyboarding (explaining) seeks to discover root causes of failures and improvement strategies by performing a metaphorical autopsy of a selling situation that produced an unwanted outcome.

Modeling (examining, exchanging) targets a specific skill or task for improvement and observing a skilled expert performing it (e.g., field ride-along).

Expert Coaching (expert coaching) transfers tacit knowledge from experts to less-skilled sellers through structured dialogue and _performance in action_.

Task _Predicting_

Most B2B salespeople make five to ten calls per day. These calls provide valuable knowledge through a variety of selling scenarios. For B2C retail sales, the daily number of potential consumers is typically much higher. One way to harness tacit knowledge more quickly is through task predicting. There are many tasks where predicting can be used to build knowledge. But predicting a prospect's response or the outcome of a skill or task that you have accomplished are great to start with.

Task predicting involves:

1. Identifying a specific subtask or subskill for improvement
2. Estimating the aspect of the skill that you want to measure (e.g., time duration, prospect response, and task outcome)
3. (After performing the task) comparing the actual measure to your prediction
4. Analyzing the reasons for the "gap," evaluating new options for improvement
5. Recycling: repeating the process for a different similar task, adding any improvements or lessons learned

Example of Predicting:

The seller "Carl" has a scheduled meeting with a prospect to discuss the final terms and pricing on a new software system costing around sixty thousand dollars. He predicts the response of the prospect when the price is given. Perhaps the reaction might be to question the value of the deal to establish a leverage position for price negotiation. Once the task is completed, Carl makes a mental note of the prospect's response. He later records the notes into a CRM system or other electronic device. When Carl compares his prediction to what actually occurred, learning through analysis occurs. The goal is to increase focus and reflection to improve recall, which enables faster and more accurate future decision making.

As predicting is applied to different tasks over time, tacit knowledge can be acquired and accessed at much quicker rates. *See Table 10.4 for scheduling and planning Predicting activities.*

Task *Piloting*

Several years ago, while leading a sales district at Pitney Bowes, one of our top sales reps, Casey Perkins, wanted to improve the efficiency of her customer meetings. At one of our regional sales meetings, she learned that Paulette (a product manager sales expert), was using an electronic tool that she attributed to cutting her meeting times nearly in half. The next time Paulette was in town, Casey arranged to go over the questionnaire tool with her.

A week later, Casey came into my office, ecstatic about how she had just left a client meeting and how the questionnaire helped her control her meeting times better. She started using the tool regularly, which made it even more effective for her work. As a result, I asked her to roll it out to other advanced members of the sales team. The electronic questionnaire tool became part of Casey's success routine after it had already been in practice with Paulette. In this example, we learn how piloting can be used to make routine tasks much better.

By using task piloting as an ongoing improvement, salespeople speed up skill growth and avoid hitting the wall. Varied routines also build stronger mental models that drive the development of expertise. Consider the following process for task piloting:

1. Identify a specific task, strategy, or method that you want to pilot. (Tasks from other top-skilled performers make good sources for new tasks.)
2. Perform the task.
3. Reflect on how the new task may have impacted the sale (immediate feedback).
4. Perform additional trials. Try the new task in other similar scenarios to compare the impact to the previous task. Additional trials are also important to ensure that the performance of the new task is smoother to make a fairer comparison.
5. Decide whether or not to adopt. Based on the feedback you gather, decide if you will use the new task permanently, not at all, or conditionally.

Task piloting can also be used with task predicting. For instance, you may want to pilot a new task or skill, then predict the outcome or the prospect's response.

In many sales cultures, peer-to-peer competition or other factors can lead to silos that limit idea sharing. Task piloting represents the low-hanging fruit of PBL as sellers have the opportunity to share and learn from other experts. According to Fadde and Klein's article: *Deliberate Performance: Accelerating Expertise in Natural Settings*, "experimenting (task piloting) is one of the most important learning processes we engage in." Piloting should be done regularly as it creates more opportunities for learning surprises, which fosters continued growth.

Piloting as a Structured Activity

Piloting should be worked into your sales planning process at least once per quarter. *See Table 10.4 for scheduling and planning Piloting activities.*

Call Reflection

Example of Post-Call Reflection:

A B2B salesperson named "Jack" sells pharmaceutical drugs to physicians and hospitals. Jack just ended a sales meeting with Dr. Jenkins regarding switching from a competitor's drug to Jack's Zytenol X product. The purpose of the meeting was to qualify a trial for the new medication. Drug trials typically consist of free giveaway samples of a new medication to the prescribing doctor. To achieve this, Jack needed to ask questions about Dr. Jenkins's practice and patient needs. Now, as he heads back to his car, Jack is unsure of how the call went. The doctor answered his questions and provided important input regarding his practice. But he was hesitant to commit to testing the drug with his patients. The meeting lasted twenty-five minutes.

Jack sits in his car and replays the dialogue in his head. He tries to answer the question as to the reason Dr. Jenkins was hesitant to pilot the new drug. Looking through his shorthand notes, he remembers that the doctor seemed to initially agree to the trial before reversing his thoughts. Jack focuses on the moments before the doctor expressed concern over the drug. He recalls showing a chart that indicated that most patients had experienced no side effects from the drug. At that moment, Dr. Jenkins responded, "Some of those reports are set up to say whatever they want them to." Jack reacted by sort of laughing off the doctor's comment and responding, "Yeah I know, but this one is not going to cause your patients any problems." As Jack reflects on this part of the dialogue he reasons that Dr. Jenkins became skeptical about the data supporting the limited side effects of Zytenol X. When Jack failed to properly recognize Dr. Jenkins's concern, the doctor pushed back and decided to wait for more data.

In this example, Jack had detected the issue when he laughed it off, but he never connected with the doctor's concern. He could have asked additional clarifying questions that may have allowed him to resolve the matter. Also, Jack wondered if by showing the chart when he did, if his bad timing may have triggered the concern. This learning may lead Jack to piloting a revised presentation that could improve the transition to the chart. Such an improvement might present the side effects data in a more positive light, reducing the chance of raising a red flag. Jack has also deposited knowledge by recognizing that an ill-advised proof source can create a negative perception for the buyer, which could lead to an objection.

As you can see in this example, there are key intuitive decisions made throughout a sales dialogue, any of which could have a lethal or positive effect on the sale. By thinking reflectively, you harness more tacit knowledge in less time while limiting errors in future engagements.

Call reflection helps to create new patterns of intuitive thinking. It involves intentional thirty-second pauses of thinking before and after sales calls.

Pre-call reflection occurs just *before* engaging in a face-to-face or online visual interaction. It primes knowledge for the pending discussion. This is a great opportunity to recall similar situations you have experienced. We know that lessons learned act as a prompt to avoid repeating them. If you're working to improve a skill, you can think through each aspect of executing it before your meeting. When pre-call reflection becomes a routine activity, you are effectively exercising intuitive skills in your daily work.

Post-call reflection occurs immediately *after* the sales call (or as soon as possible). The primary goal is to examine the task performed looking for cause and effect actions. The central idea of call reflection is to replay thinking to pinpoint tacit knowledge used for intuitive decision making. Reflective learning improves cognitive awareness while priming knowledge for future selling situations.

Notes as Triggers

Using shorthand notes is a simple thing you can do to build reflective knowledge. A few years ago, a young sales rep named Drew came to my office to discuss his e-commerce services with me. As I answered his questions, I noticed Drew's note taking. He was close enough where I could actually see what he wrote. He used headers, circled key points, and drew arrows. As the conversation went on, I saw that he was capturing the essence of our talk with great skill. As we concluded, I asked him how he used his notes. He indicated that at the end of each day, he referred to them to make sure that he kept all of his customer information well organized. I could see how his notes became a valuable asset for recalling events and growing his knowledge faster than the norm. Some people have better memories than others, but taking good notes is an essential skill for anyone in sales.

Call Reflection as a Structured Activity

Call reflection should be a part of your daily sales process and applied to your key sales calls. *See Table 10.4 for scheduling and planning Call Reflection activities.*

Storyboarding

> *"Failure is not fatal but failure to change might be."*
> **—John Wooden**

Storyboarding the Undesirable Sales Outcome

Recall in Chapter 2, the case story involving the $1.2 million dollar sale where my sales team leveraged lessons learned from a previous failure which led to a much improved team selling process. These types of situations are great examples of storyboarding. The following is a summary of that storyboarding activity:

1. After a subpar selling performance, we gathered in a room with a large whiteboard to figure out what went wrong and how to improve.
2. We diagrammed the sales scenario on the board, which gave us a clearer picture of the tasks that we needed to examine. Once documented, the team found it much easier to identify and isolate root causes.
3. We highlighted the root causes.
4. We used brainstorming to generate an improved team selling process.

Effective brainstorming helps to unpack tacit knowledge from team members. It is a wise idea for sales managers to have some form of storyboarding activity in place. This allows the process itself to be improved over time, making it more valuable for stakeholders.

Professionals are constantly looking for ways to improve performance, such as learning from previous experience and through observing others. Storyboarding is a reflective learning activity designed to leverage past experiences for future improvement. The storyboard most of us are familiar with relates to explaining the sequences of a movie or video production. Like this traditional process, sales storyboarding involves a documented activity used to evaluate experiences for improvement. It can be done using very simple to complex problem-solving models and tools. The type of model used is based on the scope and size of the project. The activity can be applied by a solo salesperson or a team. Storyboarding is used proactively or reactively as follows:

- Ongoing self-improvement (Proactive)
- In the wake of an unwanted sales outcome (Reactive)

Proactive Storyboarding

When something bad happens, there is more of a natural inclination to try to fix the problem to prevent it from happening again. However, when it comes to improvement, lessons learned can come through many other experiences. These can include your own successes and the success of other exemplary performers. The central idea of proactive storyboarding is to create a mindset of continuous improvement. Salespeople use it to analyze predicting, piloting, and call-reflection activities looking for new ways to improve. For example, let's say an office equipment sales rep wanted to improve her forecasting accuracy. In self-analysis, she finds that she's missing her sales forecast by 23 percent. A storyboarding forecast exercise might involve drilling down on every account forecasted in the past year. She could compare accounts that were closed with accounts that did not. The differences between desired and undesired aspects reveal the improvement window for forecasting.

Multiple PBL activities can be used in concert to provide deeper insights into performance. Consider task piloting, where reflective learning creates opportunities for storyboarding. A salesperson could employ reflection to understand why a pilot may have worked or not. This could also lead to new insights in other areas that may be suitable for improvement. Last, as a result of call reflection, storyboarding may be used for situations that require a more in-depth analysis. In essence, proactive thinking helps to determine how to best improve the performance of a task or skill.

In most applications of storyboarding, teams or groups will typically engage in the activity. However, as was the case with the preceding forecast example, sales reps can also engage on their own. The essence of storyboarding is assessing the current method to find flaws that need to be improved. In my experience, 80 percent of the battle is taking the first step (deciding to review the targeted task). Many times, the flawed seller is actually capable of generating viable solutions once he decides that improvement is needed.

At times, you might benefit from the insights from an outside source to help you pinpoint areas for improvement. You may want to ask your sales manager or a trusted advisor to weigh in. It should be noted that one solution may not be the only way of solving the problem. Solutions vary among skilled performers but the constant in expertise is striving for new learning and improvement.

Tools and Tips for Storyboarding

For storyboarding, it's good to have a facilitator guide the conversation and solicit input from the group. Problem-solving models and tools can also be used to provide a framework that is consistent and reliable. You can use Google and other search engines to find different models and tools on the internet. I've also placed two popular problem-solving models in the appendix section of this book. There are no hard rules or procedures that work for everyone, but the ensuing guidelines may help make storyboarding as productive as possible:

- For groups, appoint or nominate a meeting facilitator.
- Appoint or nominate a scribe to capture the group's feedback.
- Narrow down and isolate the most problematic areas.
- Ask questions that reveal intuitive recognition and decision-making rationale.
  - ○ Examples: Do you recall *what you were thinking* when the customer asked about the alternative service?
  - ○ Example: Did anyone notice *how the customer reacted* to the demonstration of the (feature) name?
  - ○ Were there any *missed signals* that could have indicated the prospect was shopping for a better price?
- Once an issue has been isolated, try to pull out implicit knowledge from others (peer interrogation) by reflecting on similar occurrences from the past where a successful outcome was produced
- Whenever possible, probe other top performers or skilled subject-matter experts for additional insights on ways to improve the task

Storyboarding as a Structured Activity

In a perfect world, storyboarding would be a part of every company's standard operating procedures. But in reality, this is not the case for many organizations. If your company does not have a process in place, you may want to suggest that management give it a shot. Perhaps a one-off storyboarding session can serve as a test to see if it makes sense for your team. In addition to failed outcomes, reflective learning from near misses offers a powerful way to heighten learning. Near misses involve imagining that an error could have a worst-case effect on the sale than it actually does. As a result, you correct the error even though the impact was not fatal. Learning from mistakes is an excellent source for proactive storyboarding, especially in team-selling environments. It is important to address fatal and near-fatal failures whenever possible as well as apply proactive storyboarding to prevent them from ever occurring.

See Table 10.4 for scheduling and planning Storyboarding activities.

An Example of Modeling on a Field Ride-along

My first sales job was in Houston, Texas, with a start-up office supply company called International Business Consumables (IBC). The owner, Ben Wiley, hired me and he quickly became my mentor, someone who taught me invaluable lessons on business and selling. Since I had no outside sales experience, Ben decided to take me out and show me the ropes. He was a former IBM twenty-year polished sales vet that exuded confidence whenever he walked into a sales meeting.

One day Ben decided to take me along on an appointment with a small software company in southwest Houston. It was 1986, and I remember walking into the modest office and greeting a tough-minded manager. I describe her as tough because of her very aggressive approach on price negotiation. Suddenly I was seeing a pro in his element discussing a price negotiation with a very shrewd buyer. My eyes seemed to be bulging as they darted back and forth from Ben to the buyer during their exchange. I vividly remember Ben smiling while quietly refusing to lower his price. Although he stood firm, his posture was gentle and empathetic. After coming to a stalemate, Ben quietly said, "What can we do to earn your business?" The manager replied, "Well, I'm sure you're giving these large corporations much bigger discounts than me. Just because we're not that big shouldn't cause us to have to pay more …" Ben seemed to understand and at that moment, he connected with the manager. He stated that our pricing plans were based on the margin from each particular distributor and that we did not offer large corporations any more than the small mom-and-pop companies. He went on to explain how his business was a small business and how he was committed to serving all businesses, especially smaller ones. The manager was nodding and tracking with Ben's every word. She ended up signing an order and both had huge smiles on their faces.

I was struck by Ben's calmness under pressure, so much so that later I drilled him on questions regarding the negotiation. His answers included keys to negotiation such as knowing your floor number, which is the point where you are willing to walk away from the deal. He also stated that his first priority was to make sure that he completely understood the buyer's concerns. But the implicit takeaways were never really explained, yet they reflected his expertise the most. Ben's tone, body language, and expressions all resonated in my mind. His attentiveness to the buyer's message allowed him to uncover her true concern—being respected in terms of receiving the same competitive prices as larger companies. Later, I found myself mirroring his behaviors when I made my own sales calls. The negotiation ended with both sides essentially getting what they wanted. Ben gave a small discount, which was countered with an agreement for the buyer to provide a testimonial letter.

By the way, that little software company has since grown into the giant $6.9-billion tech company that is BMC Software. Likewise, within two years, we grew IBC from Ben's garage to a $1.5-million business. My suggestion for excellent modeling opportunities is to seek out top performers in your organization and observe them in their performance setting. You may have to drive a few hours or even take a flight, but if you are well prepared, the trip will be worth it.

Ride-alongs are a staple activity in B2B sales aimed at modeling desired behaviors for novice sellers. By observing experts in their live environment, novices learn about behavior patterns in real time.

Likewise, in B2C retail, a novice new-hire often shadows a seasoned performer through on-the-job training. These activities can play a key role in building strong implicit skills. However, PBL modeling focuses on a specific skill or task that is pre-identified before the activity. The targeted tasks are narrowly focused on areas of intuitive ability and recognition. Modeling involves learning from the way experts *think* not necessarily by what they *do*.

In real-world selling we do not have the benefit of video to evaluate sales calls. However, salespeople must ask pointed questions of the expert to expose implicit knowledge. B2B field ride-alongs and sales B2C shadowing make for excellent opportunities for modeling. While the observer may be able to pick up other knowledge when observing the expert, the targeted task remains the biggest priority of the modeling activity. Consider the following guidelines for performing task modeling:

1. Identify and isolate the specific skill or task you want to improve.
2. (As often as possible) arrange for a field ride-along (or store shadowing) where the targeted skill can be executed with repetition.
3. Observers should be aware of what to look for and know how to ask interrogative cognitive-based questions of the expert.

Modeling as a Structured Activity

See Table 10.4 for scheduling and planning modeling activities.

Expert Coaching

In sports and music, coaching is heavily relied upon by those who engage in deliberate practice. Coaches design the right practice, give immediate feedback (error correction), and monitor performance. Given the vast amount of practice activity in these settings, the role of an expert coach is essential for success. In professional sales, the role of the sales manager is most often as the advisor coach. However, sales managers may or may not be skilled enough to guide advanced sellers toward expertise. So how do you know if your sales manager or supervisor is an expert coach? The answer: It doesn't really matter. When leveraging another person's tacit knowledge, the criteria for expertise is this: Possess superior skills and knowledge. That said, the best coaches not only possess relevant knowledge, they know how to explain it in simple terms. The better news is that aspiring sales experts have the ultimate control over their own coaching activity.

Within the context of PBL, the seller learns to self-coach and access useful knowledge from subject-matter experts whenever possible. It's natural for the sales manager to perform the role of coach. However, both the manager and the sales rep must focus on the seller's improvement to create the favorable conditions for expert coaching. Most sales managers and reps talk throughout the course of the day by phone or in passing in the local place of business. In the case of B2C reps, sales managers are often accessible throughout the store most days of the selling week.

Even if you have access to a skilled sales manager, the amount of time you can spend together is usually a fraction of your total selling time. Therefore, salespeople should optimize expert coaching during informal interactions with skilled performers by asking pointed questions for specific situations.

Self-Coaching

A central tenet of PBL is self-coaching. In the traditional training paradigm, this may seem counterintuitive. We naturally think of a coach as the trusted sales manager or mentor who is there to constantly provide guidance and feedback. However, expert coaching doesn't have to come from someone directing the activity. As I referenced earlier, most salespeople work alone the majority of the time. To optimize implicit learning, salespeople teach themselves using reflective activities and by asking structured questions (of experts). In contrast to deliberate practice in sports or music, filtering feedback for self-coaching presents much more of a challenging task. Therefore, you must learn to analyze and evaluate feedback in order to adopt useful input and disregard unnecessary information. By reflecting on what works and what doesn't (**pattern recognition**), the filtering process becomes easier with time.

Experts often dread questions from novices because they often lack focus and can become frustrating to answer. Self-coaching involves laser targeting of the expert's thinking through the use of questions that are brief and pointed. For instance, an observer might ask the expert questions about an observed action (or nonaction) that struck them as surprising during the observation. These questions should be asked as concisely as possible, based on the availability of the coach. Sellers can enhance the dialogue effectiveness with expert coaches using the *Structured Dialogue for Expert Coaching Model* as shown in (Figure 8.3). This tool serves as a mental roadmap to guide your questions toward the goal of revealing implicit knowledge from experts and coaches.

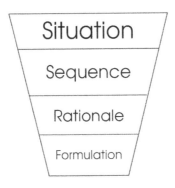

Figure 8.3 Structured Dialogue for Expert Coaching

Situation—Questions that explore the expert's situation awareness and recognition.

Examples:

- What made you think it was a (*blank*) situation?
- How did you know to (*blank*)?
- What were you thinking at the moment of (*blank*)?

Sequence—Questions that explore the order of decisions the expert should make and actions the expert should take and why he or she took them in that manner.

Examples:

- Explain why you did (*blank*) first?
- What could have happened had you not done (blank)?
- What might have changed your decision sequence if the situation were different?

Rationale—Questions that explore the reasoning the expert had for making his or her decisions.

Examples:

- Why did you decide to (*blank*)?
- Describe your thinking when you decided to (*blank*).
- Why did you rule out (*blank*) or decide not to (*blank*) instead?

Formulation—Questions that extract tacit knowledge on how the expert arrived at his thinking or conclusion.

- How did you come up with that solution?
- How long did it take you to come up with that?

- What factors led you to your conclusion?

Settings for Expert Coaching

Coaching often occurs in formal and informal settings. Sales managers and reps may regularly engage in structured meetings to discuss various topics. Field ride-alongs or shadowing activities offer the most opportune time for coaching. Many organizations have formal procedures where sales managers routinely meet with reps. Where possible, PBL coaching should be included in these discussions.

Coaching can also take place during random, informal interactions if the trainee is properly prepared. A quick run-in at the office water cooler can be a good time to engage an expert. The aspiring expert can take advantage of these informal moments by staying well prepared to ask questions. Well-prepared (structured) questions aid in extracting implicit expertise. The acquired knowledge can then be applied to your own repertoire of tacit knowledge and experiences.

Expert Coaching as a Structured Activity

To extract tacit knowledge from experts, engage in objective dialogue as often as possible. This form of self-coaching is a key element of PBL and must be primed for instant access at any given time.

See Table 10.4 for scheduling and planning on expert coaching activities.

VIDEO INTERACTIVE PRACTICE
"ANYTIME" IMPLICIT LEARNING

I n baseball, science is playing a key role in helping players improve batting performance. Dr. Peter Fadde's groundbreaking research on pitch recognition helps batters improve their hitting using empirical procedures. For example, occlusion techniques, which test the athlete's recognition, are also commonly used in sports science studies. However, Fadde repurposes them for baseball training. The tests reveal, at the earliest points of the pitch motion (just before the ball is released from the pitcher's hand), that experts show a distinct advantage over novices. These studies support the notion that expertise is often rooted in the recognition aspects of performance. During the pitch sequence, superior hitters are able to see cues that help them determine the type of pitch. Novices, on the other hand, fail to notice these same cues.

Fadde's work led to his partnering with Axon Sports, a sports training company, to create a video-based training app for baseball players. Using the app, a player learns to detect pitch types on his laptop, iPad, or smartphone versus traditional batting practice at a baseball park or batting cage. The app entails a video clip of a pitcher (from a batter's point of view) going through his pitching motion. During the motion, the screen suddenly cuts to black. At the blackout point, users are presented with multiple-choice options where they choose the pitch type (i.e., fastball, curve, or change-up). Remedial feedback is immediate, informing the player whether his answer was correct. If the chosen answer is incorrect, the correct type of pitch is revealed. Last, the video digitally cues up for the next repetition. In minutes, the pitch recognition app delivers hundreds of repetitions, helping to speed up skill development.

The study's results were eye opening. Players who engaged in the drills outperformed other players in batting average by an average of plus eighty-seven points in post-training games ($p < .05$). On-base and slugging percentages were also much higher than the control group. Another huge benefit of the training was that players could see thousands more video pitches as compared to regular forms of batting practice. Like the players of America's favorite pastime, salespeople too can systematically improve connecting skills using Video Interactive Practice™ (VIP).

The Research behind VIP

The success of pitch recognition in baseball and VIP in sales raises the question, "What is the science that makes recognition training work?" We find the answer in Fadde's Expert-Based Training (XBT), a unique training approach that evolved from the forty years of expert performance research. VIP was created using XBT instructional design and deliberate-practice training principles. The emergence of XBT adoption can be largely attributed to its architect, Dr. Fadde. In addition to following research on expertise in natural settings, he is a leading expert on training design. Expertise research by cognitive psychologists has uncovered some of the sources of experts' ability to size up situations and anticipate developments. XBT aims to systematically improve these skills, which often seem to be intuitive to both experts and those observing them. The challenge, and opportunity, comes in applying XBT principles to training expertise in different areas of performance, including sales.

As we continue the journey toward expertise, we now turn to implicit learning and connecting skills. Given that most sales training targets behavioral skills, companies typically employ whole-task training to achieve this goal. Whole-task relates to the training approach that attempts to transfer complete and complex skills to the learner. As a result, whole-task instruction offers optimum value to learners in the early stages of professional learning.

Most of these training programs are designed featuring declarative knowledge aimed at behavioral skill outcomes. For example, a seller might undergo a skills course on *How to Qualify a Prospect* or an online module on *How to Apply the ABC Qualifying Process*. These behavior-based courses can often last several days. VIP, however, targets cognitive-based implicit skills that differ as follows:

- *Brief, repetitive, and on-demand.* This approach features short, targeted repetitions delivered via smartphones and other Internet devices.
- *Implicit learning skills.* VIP drives the intuitive aspects of performance (versus skill execution). These skills are found to be most responsible for naturalistic expertise. Implicit learning involves little or no instruction, high repetition, and immediate feedback.

- *Part-task and subskills.* VIP is designed to pinpoint tasks and skills that most represent the window of expert advantage.

Fadde and other XBT instructional designers leverage expert-novice laboratory methods by repurposing them for training. As mentioned earlier, the instructional design approach of VIP evolves from laboratory techniques. For example, researchers often use expert/novice alignment methods by observing the difference in outcomes after the same task has been performed. This method is an example of how science is used to create implicit training apps.

Although VIP has a science base, the apps have the look and feel of video games. A VIP learning task (video clip) depicts a sales situation before pausing to allow the user to recognize an important aspect of the clip. The correct answers have been precoded by experts, meaning the best answers align with those given by expert subjects during app trials. Users then compare their answers with the correct (expert) answers which helps cultivate implicit learning.

Anytime learning has become the preferred learning method for many of today's sales organizations. The growth of smartphones and other devices continue to expand the portable platform, allowing salespeople to learn in between activities or during downtime. VIP is an innovative app tool that enables users to isolate and practice critical subskills anytime using these common Internet devices. These structured practice drills feature the deliberate practice elements of high repetition, progressive difficulty, and coaching feedback.

Whole-task (explicit) training usually involves large amounts of dedicated time for trainee groups. In contrast, VIP apps are available to any person anytime. Hence, the pressing question becomes, "What other ways can salespeople speed up expertise while reducing field disruptions?" Many advanced sellers find themselves at the crossroads of *needing to improve skill* and *no time for training*. Enter VIP *Implicit* skills training.

Instructional Methods of VIP

With our quest to improve vital perceptual skills, the goal is not to try to train them explicitly, but rather to set the conditions for implicit learning. Our central aim is to detect meaningful cues and messages, thus allowing your Spidey-sense to react aptly. In the words of Fadde, "We may not know exactly *what* it is, but we know *where* it is … the science has located it for us" (the window of expert advantage). It is therefore crucial to isolate and develop connecting skills apart from whole-task training.

VIP training is a timely answer for the elusive, and much needed, implicit learning. Some people might assume that selling is not a rapid decision-making environment worthy of recognition training, but selling engagements involve fast-changing dynamic communication. As noted earlier, thought-to-language sequences occur in milliseconds. Hence, sales connecting must also flow rapidly, and requires fluent cognitive reactions. As mentioned earlier, quick access of tacit knowledge is central to the expert's advantage. Said another way, the advanced seller might have much of the same knowledge as the expert, but he does not access it fast enough when needed.

Another notable benefit of VIP is the low cost of training delivery. Salespeople can learn connecting skills outside of the classroom twenty-four hours a day. Immersive whole-task training, on the other hand, will often carry large price tags that fail to achieve a return on training investment (ROTI). Costs can also be cut by replacing expensive video role plays with simulated representative tasks (rep tasks). Rep tasks are gamelike simulations that act as the key subskills most responsible for the skill being trained.

With the growth of mobile devices expected to continue, mobile learning is quickly becoming the new platform of choice for the modern sales professional. Moreover, on-demand learning will continue to play a major role in how people learn in the twenty-first century.

Leveraging Video in VIP Training

The use of video has been a valuable tool in sales training for many years. It's often used in natural settings to enable learning through practice. Exemplary sales performers are often featured in video-based training, known as *expert-model feedback*. This modeling approach can be delivered through VIP. With expert-model feedback, participants compare their own observations to that of the experts rather than have a coach direct them in what to look for. Expertise-model feedback is designed to improve skills through observation.

Notably, unlike teaching, medicine, and other domains, field video is almost non-existent in sales due to customer privacy concerns. VIP remedies this limitation by converting research methods into rep tasks for training purposes. XBT expert Fadde asserts that, "Video-based tasks simulate decision making aspects of expert performance based on key recognition scenarios found within the (selling) environment." VIP apps are therefore designed to drill the recall, detection, and interpretation and response of recognition tasks.

Video Interactive Practice™

We now take a closer look at VIP and its unique training apps. As noted earlier, deliberate practice is designed to target specific skills for improvement. Likewise, VIP apps isolate and train targeted cognitive skills that influence intuitive expertise. As shown in (figure 9.1), VIP consists of two types of applications: 1) VIP Skill Practice and 2) VIP *Implicit* Skill Practice.

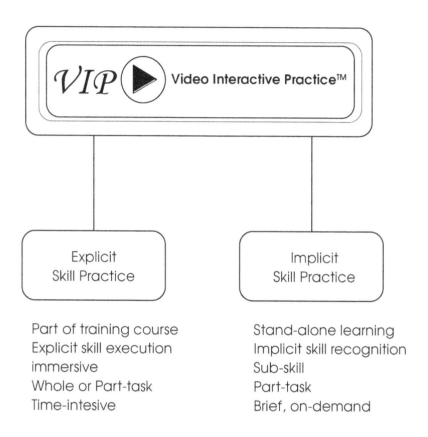

Figure 9.1 VIP Training Types–Explicit and Implicit Skills

VIP *Implicit* Skill Practice

Aspiring sales experts looking to speed up expertise must find ways to improve their implicit knowledge and skill. VIP *implicit* apps help achieve this goal by employing the train-the-brain concept of intuitive learning. These apps feature brief learning tasks that last just seconds. Unlike VIP explicit skill practice, implicit apps are directly available to the salesperson.

The VIP apps design framework includes:

1. Identifying high-impacting recognition subtasks and subskills
2. Converting recognition tasks into a training activity (rep tasks)
3. Leveraging everyday Internet tools to deliver on-demand high repetitions of implicit learning that are accessible twenty-four/seven.
4. Measuring the skill improvement and transfer using feedback and gamification tracking.

Thus, VIP implicit apps are designed to focus on the following perceptual aspects of intuitive expertise:

- Recall and Detection (Recognition)
- Categorization (Interpreting)
- Reaction and Predicting (Responding)

Recall and detection skills involve watching a vignette clip and looking for useful cues and context, then responding to a multiple choice answer prompt.

Recognition Example:

A simulated prospect makes a facial gesture and verbal response. Given a particular situational context, the user picks the answer that best describes whether the gesture requires further attention and why: choose A, B, or C.

Interpreting skills focus on making sense of the recognized message. Users respond to a multiple-choice option that best reflects the inferred meaning.

Interpreting Example:

During a price negotiation, the customer gives a vague signal such as, "We do not need anything too elaborate and would prefer a shorter finance term than the one proposed." This could best be interpreted as: choose A, B, or C.

Reaction and predicting tasks are designed to improve responsive skills and intuitive decision making. They hone in on timing decisions and whether or when the received information should be addressed. However, reaction and predictive tasks stop short of generating solutions. As noted earlier, solutions are not the focal point of VIP because experts tend to produce different remedies for the same issue or problem.

Reaction Example:

You have detected and interpreted a concern over the technical complexities of using a product during the qualifying stage. Your choices are to: respond now, respond later, or do not respond.

It should be noted that the response selections by the user are time driven to create a more realistic interaction. Once an answer is chosen, VIP provides remedial feedback to the user. Immediate feedback is a key function of VIP that drives self-learning. Conversely, with routine experience, you may have to go through many trial-and-error episodes before you learn to improve. But VIP feedback speeds advanced skill much like the GPS speeds arrival to a destination. Like the drills themselves, repetitive feedback creates new tacit thinking patterns that move you closer toward expertise. You will learn more about how to access VIP apps in the final chapter of this book.

VIP Progressive Difficulty and Gamification Features

If you have ever played online video games, you're familiar with features where the game gets harder as you increase levels. Likewise, VIP tasks increase in rigor by changing elements of the scenario or adding new information. These changes enhance situation awareness by strengthening pattern-recognition skills. Gamification features such as points, levels of achievement, progress bars, and personal best scores play an integral role in the VIP experience. The gamelike interface provides a fun learning experience and fosters optimum levels of engagement.

VIP Explicit Skill Practice

VIP explicit skill practice is designed to work along with whole-task training courses. The central idea is to drive skill transfer to the job through drill and practice. An existing curriculum must be modified to work properly with VIP. Drills are carefully designed after isolating the most critical skills that impact performance. Once the trainee has a finished drill script and a cued-up webcam, VIP recording is set to begin.

Trainees record themselves while performing a scripted sales dialogue. The brief scripts range from ten to ninety seconds and are uniquely written to train up specific subskills. Typically, trainees will engage in dialogue with a peer or supervisor acting as the prospect. The recorded videos are then uploaded to a private YouTube or similar account where an expert coach reviews them and gives feedback. After receiving feedback, the trainee records another take, correcting any errors before resubmitting a new video. Each video take is improved until it is performed at the desired level.

VIP practice is different from regular role-play because it's performed without an audience. Moreover, since drills are designed to isolate subskills, video takes have much shorter durations. Next, we will expand our discussion by learning how VIP can be used to improve whole-task training.

Enhancing Whole-Task Training

Up until this chapter, my message has been mainly geared toward sales reps and managers, the frontline revenue creators who directly drive sales. We now include as part of our audience those professionals who sponsor or put on sales training. Our aim is to help make sure that your training delivers a meaningful impact to your organization's performance and results. While conventional training activity may be down, it hasn't completely disappeared. Many sales organizations have reduced the amount of training, in part, to avoid disruptions to the sales force. This raises the question many organizations are asking: "How do we ensure our training has impact and remains relevant to our audience?"

According to the Association Society of Training and Development's 2013 State of Sales Training report, US companies spent over twenty billion dollars on sales training in 2012. Most of these training programs are geared for salespeople tenured less than three years. Moreover, selling skills and product training make up 60 percent of sales training events, which points to a predominant instructor-led industry. The study also suggests that advanced sellers learn mostly from peers, mentors, and coaches. Notably, salespeople with ten years or more experience engage in less than one week of training per year. This data supports the notion that advanced sellers do not view existing training as a means of moving to the next level.

Training professionals want to meet their ROTI and performance goals with minimal disruptions to field selling. A key aspect of a modernized training strategy should therefore include mobile tools that drive performance. This blended learning approach helps to leverage programs like VIP to enhance existing whole-task training. Moreover, VIP implicit apps can be used to improve the personal skills of advanced reps. In short, video-based practice is a powerful way to improve whole-task learning and transfer. Consider the ensuing six enhancements which address the inherent problems found in traditional training:

1. (Pre-training) *Skill assessments* highlight personal skill gaps so that training is designed and delivered as needed. Current skill level is also factored in the design of VIP. Drills can be personalized and set just above the current skill level of the student.

2. (Pre-training) Optimize training content in part by *identifying subskills* that most influence the desired performance. Subskills

are parts of whole-task skills that are carefully analyzed and broken down into specific tasks. Each subskill chunk is organized in a logical pattern-based order to optimize fluid repetition. The remaining declarative training content should be moved into e-learning, revised or removed from the training altogether.

3. (During Training Event) The ratio of practice time compared to nonpractice is optimal when 75 percent of training is practice and 25 percent lecture and other delivery methods.

4. (After Training Event) Trainees receive a detailed practice plan along with prescribed VIP drills and reflective learning activities.

5. (After Training Event) A level three or four or predictive evaluation should be done at a designated time after the training event. The evaluation provides the organization with a report that shows the impact of training compared to the performance goals.

6. (After Training Event) The training instructor, or skilled coach, provides accurate and timely feedback to the student to find and correct errors. In addition, other forms of support are provided to make sure that skills are transferred to the job.

Addressing these six areas makes excellent starting points in your training evaluation process. Through these enhancements, sales organizations can better evaluate, improve, and measure training impact and ROTI. Management should also work closely with salespeople to make sure the training meets their learning needs.

VIP Explicit Learning to Enhance Whole-Task Training

An effective tool to enhance skills training is to adopt VIP to drive and practice and reinforce practice for students. These enhanced additives create favorable conditions to achieve your learning and performance goals. By modifying existing curriculum, good courses can be made better using VIP. Sales managers can also integrate VIP into training follow-up using Skype, Google+, and other similar networking sites. The idea is for the sales manager, who acts as the customer, to assign a script for the sales rep to practice before the video conference. The manager acts as the prospect. VIP skill practice can be done online from different remote locations or in the same room. Using live two-way video, sales managers can observe sales presentations and other action-based skills. Using a webcam or recording feature, video is recorded and saved for further analysis. The recorded video is then analyzed by both the sales rep and the manager for reflective feedback. These forms of two-way live video are also very useful for salespeople who work in remote locations from their manager. Video training enhances knowledge exchange and coaching feedback far beyond the limits of phone conversations.

As we have discussed, using VIP involves identifying the targeted subskills for practice. First, a certified VIP designer can assist in reformatting training material. Second, dialogue scripts are created from your course content. Third, the drills are practiced during and after training workshops when recorded videos are submitted. For new training programs still under development, it's a good idea to consider writing VIP into the training design.

VIP Implicit Skill Training to Enhance Whole-Task Training

Although implicit training is not meant to replace whole-task skills training, it can be used to enhance it. One of the inherent problems with traditional training is *information dump*, where the trainee is overwhelmed with too much material. Many training courses include several whole-task skill concepts in a single course. To compound the problem, these courses don't allow enough time for practice. As a result, training is often perceived as too long and not student friendly. VIP implicit training can be used to decrease these problems in the following ways:

- Implement VIP *implicit learning as a pre-requisite* for the upcoming skills workshop. This allows learners to learn key subskills, which eases their cognitive load during the training, thereby boosting retention.
- Implement *implicit learning during the workshop* as a way to break up the training format and increase skill repetition.
- Implement *post-workshop PBL activities* during routine work to prime tacit knowledge and intuitive skill adoption. These supportive learning tasks enhance transfer, greatly improving the impact of whole-task training.

Using these expert performance training principles, VIP fuels the speed of the mental actions needed for expert selling. As companies continue to move toward *anytime* training models, VIP and PBL represent unique solutions capable of meeting your current and future learning needs.

Summary and Reflections on Section Three

- Performance-Based Learning® activities include Task "Predicting," Task "Piloting," "Call" Reflection, "Storyboarding," Task "Modeling," and Expert Coaching. These learning activities accelerate skill acquisition and expertise through routine daily work.
- VIP is constructed using XBT instructional design methods that feature deliberate practice.
- Video Interactive Practice™ *Implicit* training drives on-demand learning of critical sales connecting skills.
- VIP Explicit and *Implicit* training enhances whole-task training courses by driving on-the-job learning transfer and performance.

Chapter 10

THE BLUEPRINT
STEP-BY-STEP PLAN TO
ACCELERATE SELLING EXPERTISE

"Give me six hours to chop down a tree and I will spend the first four sharpening the axe."

—Abraham Lincoln

I am a strong believer in planning for what you want to achieve … plan your work, work your plan. A well-thought-out plan helps to guide your actions toward your goal. Moreover, part of any good sales plan should include a development component that identifies the learning you need to be successful.

One of the biggest challenges you'll face after reading this book is turning it into actionable tasks. We've all gone to that awesome training class or read the motivating book that was a great read only to continue doing the same old things. But the goal of *Expert Selling* is to infuse a new pathway to success and help salespeople get there faster. That means providing clear answers to the questions regarding improving performance and speeding expertise. That said, the content of this book is only as useful as you make it. Therefore, I urge you to carefully read through this last chapter and follow the blueprint to reach your full expert potential.

Conclusion

I hope you have enjoyed this journey as much as I've enjoyed being your driver and sharing my thoughts and insights with you. Throughout my career, I have done my best to try and make meaningful contributions to the success of business people. Whether engaged in training, thought leadership, and of course, selling, my focus remains helping you be the best that you can be.

Coach Wooden coined this definition of success: "Peace of mind, attained only through self-satisfaction and knowing you made the effort to do the best that you are capable [of]." You probably have gathered by now that I love John Wooden quotes, so it's only fitting that I share this last one. Actually, it's a poem by Glennice L. Harmon which Wooden, a former English teacher and lover of poetry, would often quote during his talks:

They Ask Me Why I Teach
By Glennice L. Harmon
They ask me why I teach,
And I reply,
Where could I find more splendid company?
There sits a statesman,
Strong, unbiased, wise,
Another later Webster,

Silver-tongued,
And there a doctor
Whose quick, steady hand
Can mend a bone,
Or stem the lifeblood's flow.
A builder sits beside him—
Upward rise
The arches of a church he builds, wherein
That minister will speak the word of God,
And lead a stumbling soul to touch the Christ.
And all about
A lesser gathering
Of farmer, merchants, teachers,
Laborers, men
Who work and vote and build
And plan and pray
Into a great tomorrow
And I say,
"I may not see the church,
Or hear the word,
Or eat the food their hands will grow."
And yet—I may.
And later I may say,
"I knew the lad,
And he was strong,
Or weak, or kind, or proud,
Or bold, or gay.
I knew him once,
But then he was a boy."

They ask me why I teach, and I reply,
"Where could I find more splendid company?"
"They Ask Me Why I Teach," by Glennice L. Harmon.[1]

Writing this book involved a lot of time and effort but because of your presence, the experience has been truly wonderful. I am confident that the ideas and concepts presented, combined with your skills, talents, and efforts, will make a positive impact on helping you achieve your goals. I hope that this book also can bring meaningful insights to your life as a whole.

Can we make everyone an expert? Probably not, but I'm certain that many of you can discover the inspiration to find new ways of trying. There are journeymen with the capability and desire to become experts, and there are many novices hungry to advance their skills. The bottom line is, there's an appetite for excellence where people are looking for better ways to achieve their success dreams. I hope the ideas and examples discussed have helped to illuminate the way.

The following is a step by step guide (blueprint) to help you move towards your goals and overall sales excellence.

Table 10.1 Expert Selling Action Plan "The Blueprint"

TASK	Description/ Rationale	DUE BY	STATUS/ NOTES
Step 1 Reread Book	I recommend reading the book at least twice to optimize understanding of the concepts and ideas.		

---

1   Glennice L. Harmon, "They Ask Me Why I Teach," NEA Journal 37, no. 1 (September 1948): 375

Step 2 Join *Expert Selling* Sales Blog	Our sales blog/ website includes a complete support tools library and other development resources. *Use QR code below*		
Step 3 Write Performance Goals	Performance goals are proven to positively impact learning and performance. They create a clear line of sight to performance improvement.		
Step 4 Identify PBL Activities Prioritize and Schedule	These unique activities enable you to accelerate expertise through your routine work.		
Step 5 Measure and Adjust	Leveraging the Expert Selling resources, you'll have real-time access to performance progress via dashboards and other metric reporting.		

Note: An electronic copy of this action plan can be accessed through the *Expert Selling* website at: *www.sales-blueprint.com*

Steps

1. *Reread Expert Selling*: Repetition and refinement are hallmarks of expert performance and are discussed throughout this book. I recommend you read the book at least twice to fully absorb the concepts and information. The first read-through should be at your normal reading pace. As you come across material that you want to refer back to, make a note or indicator for that section. By the way, please feel free to mess up the pages with markups because that is precisely how you should use the book. On the second read-through, take your time and review the content that you feel will be most important to you. This step-by-step plan coupled with your second read will help to transform words into action. I suggest a third read if you want a deeper understanding of the content or if perhaps you'd like to teach *Expert Selling* to others.

2. *Join our "Expert Selling" Blog Community*. This book earns you a free membership in our sales blog and social media network. The main goal of this virtual sales community is to provide sales professionals with real-time support and networking with other colleagues and experts. Our website is filled with great support tools that help you take your sales to

the next level. The following tools and services are included with your new membership:

REGISTER AT: *www.sales-blueprint/expert-selling-blog* or scan the QR code below.

Online Video Tutorial Library—These short video clips are packed with skill improvement insights such as the Six Essentials of Persuasive Communication as well as other *Expert Selling* topics.

Online Sales Tools—You'll find everything here from job aids from this book to proposal templates, sales-plan templates, and everything in between. These tools alone are worth the door price of admission, if you will, so make sure that you check them out.

"Ask the Sales Coach"— An expert coaching service for salespeople to assist with day-to-day selling issues. Members can submit online questions to an expert coach or interact directly using our VIP system.

Online Sales Assessment—Take our ten-minute online assessment to pinpoint your learning needs and priorities. There are different levels based on performance and experience. Your personal assessment report empowers you to work toward professional development.

Sales Certification—Our rigorous sales certification program validates your training efforts by recognizing sales acumen throughout the global sales community. We provide a formal certificate once you complete your certification requirements.

Free Online Webinars and Training—Members of our blog community receive instant access to webinars and selected online training courses. The webinars cover practical and useful topics that help you perform better while improving your skills. Members also receive priority access to our ongoing distance learning sales courses.

3. *Write Performance Goals*. As noted in Chapter 4, performance goals are interconnected to your skill-development priorities. Our website resource center offers several templates that aid in drafting well-aligned goals. The process is simple—(1) Identify and prioritize the skills you want to improve using the *Skill Inventory* list (Table 10.2 depicts a skill inventory list example), and (2) Write them into the performance goals map (Table 10.3 depicts a Performance Goal Map example). The skills from *Expert Selling* are preloaded into the template for easy completion of the performance goals map. Additional skills can be added as well using generic map templates.

Table 10.2 Example of Skill Inventory List

Persuasive Communication	Skills	Subskills
	Pausing/Silence Clarity Planning Nonverbal comm. Attentiveness Perceptiveness Responsiveness	Wait for complete response Paraphrasing Scripting Mirroring Active Listening Connecting Adapting

Table 10.3 Example of Performance Goal Map

Skill	Process Goal	Performance Goal	Outcome Goal
Effective Planning Pausing	Rehearse presentation delivery Allow time for reflection after presenting topic	Improve close ratio	Outperform quota by 10% Achieve President's Club
Skill # 2	Second Process Goal	Second Performance Goal	Second Outcome Goal (if different from first one)

4. ***Implement Performance-Based Learning® Activities.*** PBL on-the-job learning can play an instrumental role in accelerating intuitive expertise. Predicting, piloting, reflection, storyboarding, and modeling should be carefully integrated into your work routine. The key is quality, not quantity. The following structured activities chart provides suggested timing and frequency of adopting PBL into your work.

Table 10.4 Performance-Based Learning® (Structured Activities)

PBL Activities	Situation/Tasks For Activity	Timing Frequency	Additional Information
Predicting (Prospect reactions)	Response to questions Response to new job aid Duration of presentation Forecasting	One to two weekly	Focus on one task type at a time Use automated form of tracking

Task Piloting	Maintain "surprises" in selling routine Constantly seek improvement	At least one piloting activity monthly	Piloting tasks can come from successful experts. Focus on task or skill Document results
Call Reflection	Learn by doing Turn routine work into lessons learned	After each meaningful sales call	"Think about thinking" Identify cause and effect Isolate tasks
Storyboarding	High-stakes selling situation with undesired outcome	Schedule after a *catastrophic failure* event or *near miss* Schedule (quarterly) to evaluate PBL activities	Team or individual Incorporate problem-solving tools Document *lessons learned* and improvements
Task Modeling	Learn from others Observe experts in their natural settings	Whenever expert or skilled performer is accessible	Focusing on expert thinking vs. skill execution Alternative: Modeling simulations through video
Expert Coaching	Self-coaching through questioning of experts (peer interrogation)	As often as opportunities allow	Use the structured dialogue model as a guide

5. ***Download and install the VIP Implicit Learning App***. VIP sales apps target implicit learning using simple everyday tools like smartphones. More information is available through our website.

6. ***Tracking and Measuring***. All good plans must include ways to monitor progress and ensure that goals are achieved. Use this section of the plan to plot out key milestone dates and to assess your improvement. You will also find progress dashboards and other tools that automate tracking, making VIP more useful and productive.

ACKNOWLEDGMENTS

There are so many people who deserve accolades for supporting me in writing this book. First to my family: Tanya and Sedric II, thank you for your love and support during the many months of research and writing. I will always remember your sacrifices.

Thank you Rita Rosenkranz, a wonderful agent who helped give me the chance to share my work with the world.

Next, allow me acknowledge those who provided their technical expertise for the research that went into this book: Dr. K. Anders Ericsson, Dr. Peter Fadde, and Dr. Gary Klein, your wealth of academic knowledge is only matched by your willingness to take the time to share your thoughts and ideas with me. I'm honored to have had the opportunity to learn from each of you.

My hat goes off to two of the best editors in the business: Jennifer Zaczek and Amanda Rooker, thank you for guiding me through the painful journey of molding my raw ideas into a well-organized message that readers can understand and enjoy.

I am both proud and grateful to have worked with such a wonderful team at Morgan James Publishing: David Hancock, Terry Whalin, Margo Toulouse, Jessica Foldberg, and Allison Garrett. Your publishing acumen is second to none.

Major props for my colleagues, friends and mentors who constantly encourage and inspire me to be better each day: Peter Rodarte, Dave Basarab, Michael Christie, Edward Diba, Ben Wiley, Reverend Mark Whitlock, and Chuck Jackson. You've all had a major impact on not only my work–but my life as a whole. Finally, I'm grateful to have worked with so many sales experts and great business leaders at Pitney Bowes and Neopost corporations. My heartfelt thanks goes out to all of you.

Appendix

"HONORABLE MENTIONS"

I've had many sales associates, friends, and colleagues ask me to write about many other important sales subjects, so I thought I'd address a few of them here in the appendix section. These are my honorable mentions of sorts, but even though they fall outside of the main scope of this book, they represent important real-world issues that concern salespeople. I present my brief take on these important subjects in two hundred words or less, but I encourage you to contact me directly on any sales-, training-, or performance-related questions that you might have.

Appendix A
APPENDIX A—PRODUCT KNOWLEDGE (PK)

Beyond new-hire selling skills training, sales organizations invest most of their remaining training dollars into product/service related training. This includes everything from full training courses to product launches and updates. My view is that many organizations are guilty of product knowledge (PK) *overkill*. That is, they believe the more product data thrown at salespeople, the more effective they'll be at selling it.

Organizations need to be more strategic when designing product training by focusing more on the high-impact solution capabilities (Big Sexys) versus technical features. Companies with many products often confuse the sales force in part because the products are not always well categorized. Higher end, more complex products and services will continue to trend in direct sales, so it's critical to understand their high-level capabilities. It's equally important to be proficient at identifying and presenting them with clarity. I like to say expert salespeople are able to thin-slice the technical jargon, making it easier for prospects to understand. Last, to enhance effectiveness, salespeople must also master the competitor's products and identify the advantages and strengths. Effective PK is more about how products solve business issues (B2B) or quality of life (B2C) rather than spewing out features and specs.

Appendix B
BUSINESS CULTURE AND INDUSTRY KNOWLEDGE (BIK)

Today's more informed prospect often learns more about your product/service using the Internet or by networking with other users. Expert sellers must therefore develop a strong business and industry acumen that fosters adaptiveness and boosts credibility.

How do you gain the competitive advantage over your competitors? One way is to provide insights into the prospect's business and industry. Example: If you're selling computer software and calling on an insurance service provider, consider this good-to-best progression of an Initial Benefit Statement (IBS) dialogue:

Sales Rep (Novice—Good): "I'd like to talk to you about our new software product that can help you better manage your accounting and billing processes. I can arrange a demo so you can take a closer look …"

Sales Rep (Journeyman—Better): "I've been working with several insurance companies in the area talking about new claims CRM systems, which help reduce your claims and improve your billing as well …"

Sales Rep (Expert—Best): "I've been working with several clients within the risk management sector and since introducing our new claims processing solution, we're hearing that customer claim cycles are down by twenty to thirty percent while premium billings are much more accurate and timely …"

Appendix C
SALES ACTIVITY AND PIPELINE MANAGEMENT

How important is effort? In the context of normal standards of performance, effort and sales activity remain crucial. Selling skills can't impact results if the seller isn't in front of customers.

Contrary to the popular belief that selling is a sort of abstract art-form that goes up or down with the tides of chance, it is actually a fairly predictable exercise. You've all heard the infamous sales manager proclamation, "Sales is a numbers game." The manager is half-right. Selling is a numbers "business" (not a game). It's very simple arithmetic:

The results will always mirror activity. The key is to know your average revenue per order (ARPO) and your close rate (CR). Consider the activity results formula in this example:

A. Annual Quota: $1,000,000
B. Monthly Quota: $83,333 (= A ÷ 12 months)
C. Avg. Revenue Per Order: $15,000 (annual # orders ÷ total sales revenue)
D. Close Rate: 20% (Avg. percentage of prospects on 30-Day Pipeline sold annually)
E. Avg. Monthly Pipeline Required: $416,333 ($83,333 ÷ 20% CR)

So based on this sales rep's CR and ARPO, he needs to maintain an average of $416, 333 in his thirty-day *closeable* pipeline.

To determine the average number of prospects needed in the Thirty-Day Pipeline:

F. Number of monthly prospects needed: 28 (E ÷ C)

To determine how many "unqualified prospects" are needed to maintain "F:"

G. Number of "unqualified prospects:" 56 (Estimate the percentage for your industry)

To determine average number of daily sales calls needed to achieve quota:

H. Number of daily calls needed: 3 (= G ÷ 20 working days in each month)

Note: H does not include "follow-up" calls in most industries.

The flipside of activity management is that salespeople must focus on meaningful calls rather than simply calling and "bugging" prospects.

A 2010 B2B survey on sales decision makers by McKinsey & Company revealed that 35 percent of respondents felt salespeople make too many contacts in the sales process.

Appendix D
MEANINGFUL SALES LEADS

Many sales reps are concerned with the lack of quality leads generated from internal and external sources. There's several contributing factors to this: 1) The 2008 recession and subsequent recovery has rendered many businesses to continue spending restraints resulting in fewer calls for new products/services, and 2) Marketing and inside sales departments are running into this same resistance, which creates a lower standard for a qualified lead. The very definition of *lead* has begun to be used interchangeably with ***targeted unqualified prospect***, which is merely a soft lead designated to represent a worthy opportunity to check out further.

Given the fact that many sales markets have matured along with more competition, the trend of weaker external leads could likely continue. That said, organizations should focus on generating higher quality leads for salespeople by improving marketing clarity and upgrading the talent level of the inside marketing staff. At the same time, salespeople can also generate their own leads within their territory. Many organizations support and encourage their sales forces to create custom marketing messages. These types of strategies can improve lead conversion rates because they leverage the salesperson's personalized knowledge of the customer.

Appendix E
COMPETITIVE SUPPORT STRATEGIES

Twenty years ago, prospects shopped around maybe two or three times out of every ten deals. Today, in many sales industries, those numbers have reversed.

There's a wonderful business book called *Blue Ocean Strategy* (W. Chan Kim and Renée Mauborgne). The book suggests that companies should strive to move out from the blood-infested red waters where sharks (competitors) roam and instead create new blue oceans of uncontested offerings, thereby redefining your value proposition in ways that minimize or eliminate competitors.

Sellers can also create blue oceans by: 1) looking at customer needs using a more creative lens, 2) changing the traditional sales process to be more customer engaging (example, inviting prospects to informative webinars or open-house-type events), and 3) by modifying existing product and pricing configurations that best suit customer needs while excluding competitors from the playing field. For example, by analyzing different product/service combinations, you might find a niche that only your solution fits. Many times, relatively dormant product features are taken for granted, but with a little creativity they can morph into a major selling opportunity. Last, when necessary, you might have to fight fire with fire just to win the deal and create a future opportunity for the blue ocean. To put it simply, if you are selling apples (value) but the customer is buying oranges (price), sell oranges today and work on the apples for tomorrow.

Appendix F
CONSULTATIVE-SOLUTION SELLING VERSUS INSIGHT SELLING

Today's sales organizations continue to shift their sales forces toward more complex products and services. It is therefore important to discuss solution selling as compared to insight selling. Over the last few years, many sales training pundits and thought leaders have begun to advance the notion of a new method known as *insight selling*. There's an ongoing debate on whether insight selling will be responsible for sunsetting the popular *consultative-* or *solution*-selling methods. It should be noted, however, that *selling intuitively* is not a sales *method* but rather a *higher-order thinking function*. Said another way, true experts have the ability to apply their intuitive skills across virtually any sales method or process.

Insight-selling methods are characterized by selling with a judgment emphasis that disrupts the customer's beliefs. This contrasts with the traditional regimented sales process designed to align a product solution to an explicit need. Likewise, selling intuitively involves injecting new insights to influence the prospect's perspective. A notable difference is that selling intuitively is based on cognitive skills versus behavioral skills. Experts sell intuitively by leveraging tacit knowledge from previous similar sales situations and by sharing these insights with customers. Conversely, other approaches to insight selling seem to suggest that insights derive from on-demand research and fact-finding missions prior to the sales engagement. The pre-call gathering is done to arm the seller with useful insights aimed at creating prospect interest in new ideas. Pre-call research is a task-driven planning activity, and it is certainly helpful to the sales process. Expert-level salespeople routinely carry out pre-call planning whenever needed. Many sales businesses are known for overemphasizing various sales processes and activities to the point where this can drown out sales creativity. To counter this, organizations need to encourage creative ingenuity while limiting hard and fast rules that are often perceived as inflexible. My hope is that as the quest for expertise expands, we'll see more cognitive-based programs take center stage. Insight selling is definitely a refreshing approach and has value in the sales market space especially when selling to large enterprises. But expertise transcends sales methods—it is in fact the controller that guides all sales actions.

Appendix G
BUSINESS ACUMEN (BA)

As salespeople move higher to C-level executives, they must be prepared to effectively discuss executive concerns, namely business issues and objectives. For example, not enough sellers know the difference between an income statement and balance sheet. This knowledge gap makes it harder to link product benefits to the organization's financial situation. The good news is that you can learn more about business in quick, simple ways. Here are a few suggestions: 1) Ask C-level customer questions regarding their P&L (profit and loss) objectives and how they are progressing against them. Learning from actual customers in your industry better relates the information to your product/service. 2) Focus on the *big three*—financial, operational, and customer, which includes marketing, customer service, and other customer touchpoints. These tend to be the key areas that often keep C-level executives awake at night. 3) Read your prospect's corporate materials, such as annual reports, website, and industry news. Armed with this information, you can improve business acumen (BA) by framing intelligent questions using their information as a premise.

Consider the following example from the insurance industry, which shows the collected information underlined:

Sales Rep: "I see from a <u>recent news release that your company has launched a new life product targeted at middle aged customers</u>. How has this impacted your current operations in terms of new policy order volume and service, etc.?"

Appendix H
PROSPECTING

Sales prospecting relates to finding the right new sales opportunities. While the process will vary from organization to organization, fundamentally, salespeople always seem to need more high-quality prospect leads. I would add that prospecting also involves executing an effective approach dialogue that generates attention and interest.

Typically, prospects come from three sources: existing customers, nonusers, or competitive accounts. One or all of these might apply depending on the industry. For existing customers, a smart plan involves providing excellent service and expanding the reach of your product/service in the customer's business. Avoid the common line "Your product-service is obsolete," as this doesn't infer any value to the customer. Instead focus on understanding their changing needs. For nonusers the idea is to identify profiles that narrow your target list into the ideal prospect, then develop a customized approach (see *Access!* letter in Chapter 2). Competitive users require more work, but the takeaways are extremely beneficial to sales organizations because they grow organic revenue while taking away market share from competitors. Building rapport and trust is crucial, so first you should find the right contact person with whom to build a good relationship. When the time is right, learn their business needs and current vendor/products and look for strengths and weaknesses. You'll want to create a vision of change to your solution and map out steps on how to get there. Often, competitive users fear the risk of switching vendors, so adapt your selling to proactively deal with risk-averse decision making.

Appendix I
CRMS IN SALES, CREATING A WIN-WIN

Many sales organizations have invested in CRM systems for various reasons, including to improve sales productivity, marketing, information management, and customer service. The challenge, however, is getting salespeople to actually use these systems consistently. When data is missing from even a few salespeople, the total CRM's usefulness is greatly lessened.

Having been involved with several major CRM rollouts, I have seen the good, bad, and the ugly of the adoption process. The first mistake is when organizations use a threatening posture that focuses on punitive actions for sales noncompliance. This can create a negative bias, resulting in many salespeople not embracing the system. Beyond this, companies often simply don't know how to effectively articulate the benefits of the CRM to their team. Moreover, there isn't always a direct connection with the top-performing reps and CRM adoption levels.

Here are some quick tips on improving CRM adoption and making the tool an integrated, effective way you do business: 1) Organizations should be sensitive to the amount of time sales will need to transition. Prioritize the must-do CRM components and phase them in by schedule. Do not rollout the next phase until an acceptable adoption level is reached. 2) Prior to launch, design useful dashboards and reports that help sellers do their jobs better. Many times the sales division is asked to duplicate reports, which adds to their workload. This could create an adverse perception, especially if management doesn't acknowledge these challenges. 3) Salespeople should make the CRM data entry automatic and part of their daily work. Instead of having to constantly try to remember to input data into the CRM for the week, do it every morning or every night at a designated time. Better yet, some systems are now capable of enabling real-time updates from a handheld device, which makes automating entry tasks even easier.

Appendix J
RECOMMENDED BOOKS

TOPIC	BOOK TITLE	AUTHOR(S)
Selling Skills	*Mastering the Complex Sale* *The Psychology of Selling* *Perfect Selling* *Selling to V.I.T.O.* *SPIN Selling* *Selling to Big Companies* *Strategic Selling* *The Psychology of Persuasion* *The Secret of Selling Anything*	Jeff Thull Brian Tracy Linda Richardson Anthony Parinello Neil Rackham Jill Konrath Stephen Heiman, Robert Miller Robert B. Cialdini Harry Browne

Communication Sales Communication Persuasive Communication	*How to Win Friends and Influence People* *The Definitive Book of Body Language* *The Art of Persuasion* *Power of Persuasion* *The Art of Persuasive Communication* *Nonverbal Communication*	Dale Carnegie Barbara Pease, Allan Pease Bob Burg Richard Butterfield Richard Storey Albert Mehrabian
Expert Performance	*The Cambridge Handbook on Expertise and Expert Performance* *The Road To Excellence: The Acquisition of Expert Performance in the Arts and Sciences, Sports, and Games* *Development of Professional Expertise* *Talent is Overrated* *Blink* *Outliers: The Story of Success* *See What Others Don't* *The Power of Intuition*	K. Anders Ericsson et.al K. Anders Ericsson Geoff Colvin Malcom Gladwell Malcom Gladwell Gary A. Klein Gary A. Klein

I also recommend trying Lumosity.com which is a highly popular brain training website designed to strengthen core cognitive functions (memory, attention, speed, problem solving, and flexibility).

Appendix K
USEFUL TOOLS AND JOB AIDS

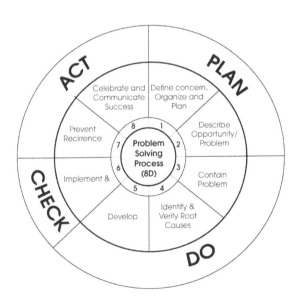

Figure 8.1 Problem-Solving Model

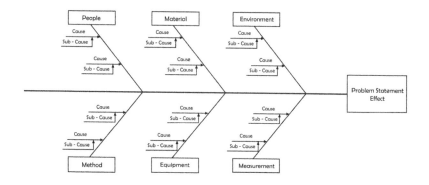

Figure 8.2 Fishbone Cause & Effect Diagram

Agenda for Proposed / Upcoming Meeting

Thank you for the opportunity to serve your (product type) needs. The following agenda is offered as a suggested guide for our proposed/scheduled meeting.

Proposed Date: February 15, 20XX

Time: 9:30 AM (1 hour)

Meeting Attendees	
ABC Sales, Inc.	XYZ Customer Name
Regina Johnson—Account Manager Rachel Glass—Technical Sales Consultant Peter Rodarte—Product Specialist Charles Patterson—Sales Manager Sedric Hill—Sales Vice President	Gary Johnson—VP Ops (Please add team members that will participate)

TIME (Estimated)	TOPIC	Discussion Leader
9:30 AM	Opening / Objectives	Regina Johnson
9:40 AM	XYZ Key Issues and Goals	Gary Johnson
9:50 AM	Solution Capabilities	Peter Rodarte
10:00 AM	Product Demo	Rachel Glass
10:20 AM	Q & A	Gary Johnson
10:25 AM	Next Steps / Actions	Gary Johnson / Sedric Hill

We welcome any additions, edits, or changes that you may have. A final agenda will be resent by (date prior to meeting).

Sincerely,

Sales Rep Name

Account Manager

XXX-XXX-XXXX (Phone)

jdoe@ABC.com (Email Address)

Special Memorial Dedication

In the introduction, you met Ed Diba, one of the most successful sales leaders I've ever known. Unfortunately, Ed passed away in February of 2013 as I was doing research for this book; but his impact on me and so many others helped inspire me to write *Expert Selling*. Ed and I shared twenty years together as colleagues and more importantly, as friends. He provided an endless source of insight to me on keys to his success, as well as the success of many other top salespeople whom he knew personally. I want to thank Ed's wife, Laura Diba, for her support of this book and her willingness to share useful aspects about Ed's illustrious career.

Ed, my friend, although you may no longer be with us in body, your dearest Laura and your twin boys carry your spirit always. In many ways, Thank you for sharing your selling expertise, your laughter, and most of all, your friendship with me and countless others. Your legacy will live on as one of the most successful sellers ever. So, until we meet again, as you'd often say…"Later, dude."

REFERENCES

Andersen, P. A., and L.K. Guerrero. 1998. *Principles of communication and emotion in social interaction*. In P. A. Andersen, ed. & L. K. Guerrero (Eds.), *Handbook of communication and emotion: Research, theory, applications, and contexts (pp. 49–96)*. San Diego, CA: Academic Press.

Bailenson, J., Yee, N. 2005. Digital Chameleons: Automatic Assimilation of Nonverbal Gestures in Immersive Virtual Environments. *The 55th International Communication Association Annual Conference*, New York, May.

Barr, Corbett. "Deliberate Practice: What Is It and Why You Need It." Web log post. *Expert Enough*. FizzleCo, Inc., 6 Feb. 2012. Web. 24 Nov. 2013. <http://expertenough.com/1423/deliberate-practice>.

Basarab, David J. 2011. *Predictive Evaluation: Ensuring Training Delivers Business and Organizational Results*. San Francisco: Berrett-Koehler.

Boaz, Nate, and John Murnane. The Basics of Business to Business-to-business Sales Success." *McKinsey & Company*. 21 Sept. 2013. <http://www.mckinsey.com/insights/marketing_sales/the_basics_of_business-to-business_sales_success>.

Boorom, Michael L., Jerry R. Goolsby, and Rosemary P. Ramsey. 1998. "Relational Communication Traits and Their Effect on Adaptiveness and Sales Performance." *Journal of the Academy of Marketing Science* 26.1 (January 1): 16-30.

Cegala, Donald J. 1981. "Interaction Involvement: A Cognitive Dimension of Communicative Competence." *Communication Education* 30: 109-21.

Collins, James C. 2001. *Good to Great: Why Some Companies Make the Leap—and Others Don't*. New York, NY: HarperBusiness.

Colvin, Geoffrey. 2008. *Talent Is Overrated: What Really Separates World-class Performers from Everybody Else*. New York: Portfolio.

Ericsson, K. Anders. 1996. *The Road to Excellence: The Acquisition of Expert Performance in the Arts and Sciences, Sports and Games*. Mahwah, NJ: Erlbaum.

Ericsson, K. Anders, Neil Charness, Paul Feltovich, P., and Robert R. Hoffman, eds. 2006. *The Cambridge Handbook of Expertise and Expert Performance*. Cambridge: Cambridge UP.

Ericsson, K. Anders, and Paul Ward. 2007. "Capturing the Naturally Occurring Superior Performance of Experts in the Laboratory: Toward a Science of Expert and Exceptional Performance." *Current Directions in Psychological Science*, Vol. 16, No. 6.

Ericsson, K. Anders., and A. Mark Williams. 2007." Capturing Naturally Occurring Superior Performance in the Laboratory: Translational Research on Expert Performance." *Journal of Experimental Psychology* Vol. 1, No. 3, 115-123.

Ericsson, K. Anders. 2008. "Deliberate Practice and Acquisition of Expert Performance: A General Overview." *Academic Emergency Medicine* 15.11: 988-94.

———, ed. 2009. *Development of Professional Expertise: Toward Measurement of Expert Performance and Design of Optimal Learning Environments.* New York: Cambridge UP.

———, ed. 1996. *The Road to Excellence: The Acquisition of Expert Performance in the Arts and Sciences, Sports, and Games.* Mahwah, N.J: Lawrence Erlbaum Associates.

Ericsson, K. Anders, Ralf T. Krampe, and Clemens Tesch-Römer. 1993. "The Role of Deliberate Practice in the Acquisition of Expert Performance." *Psychological Review* 100.3: 363-406.

Gladwell, Malcolm. 2005. *Blink: The Power of Thinking Without Thinking.* New York: Little, Brown.

Gladwell, Malcolm. 2008. *Outliers: The Story of Success.* New York: Little, Brown.

Fadde, Peter J. "Interservice/Industry Training, Simulation, and Education Conference (I/ITSEC)." I/ITSEC 2013 Conference, Peabody Orlando Hotel. Vol. Paper No. 13177. N.p.: n.p., n.d.

Fadde, Peter J., and Gary A. Klein. 2012. "Accelerating Expertise Using Action Learning Activities." *Cognitive Technology* 17.1: n. pag.

Fadde, Peter J., and Gary A. Klein. "Deliberate Performance: Accelerating Expertise in Natural Settings." *Wiley Online Library* 49.9: n. pag. 9 Oct. 2010. Web. http://onlinelibrary.wiley.com/doi/10.1002/pfi.20175/abstract

Fadde, Peter J. 2009. "Expert-Based Training: Getting More Learners Over the Bar in Less Time." *Technology Instruction, Cognition and Learning* 7: 171-97.

Huffman, Karen. 2011. *Psychology in Action, 10th Edition.* S.l.: John Wiley.

Kahneman, Daniel, and Gary Klein. 2009. "Conditions for Intuitive Expertise: A Failure to Disagree." *American Psychologist* 64.6: 515-26.

Klein, Gary A. 2003. *The Power of Intuition*. New York: Currency/Doubleday.

———. 2013. *Seeing What Others Don't: The Remarkable Ways We Gain Insights*. New York: Public Affairs.

Knight, Steve. 2004. *Winning State-Football: Program Your Mind Win the Confidence Battle*. Portland, OR: Let's Win.

Levine, Robert. 2003. *The Power of Persuasion: How We're Bought and Sold*. Hoboken, N.J: John Wiley & Sons.

Mehrabian, Albert. 2007. *Nonverbal Communication*. New Brunswick, NJ: Aldine Transaction.

Pease, Barbara and Allan Pease. 2009. *The Definitive Book of Body Language: The Hidden Message Behind People's Gestures and Expressions*. New York: Bantam Dell Pub Group.

Pettijohn, Charles E., Linda S. Pettijohn, A.J. Taylor, and Bruce D. Keillor. 2000. "Adaptive Selling and Sales Performance: An Empirical Examination." *The Journal of Applied Business Research* 16.1: np.

Priolo, Dario. "Top Needs Identified by B2B Sales Reps for Success in 2013." *Sales Training, Sales Management Training, Sales Coaching, Sales Transformation—Richardson*. N.p., 11 Jan. 2013. Web. 17 Sept. 2013. <http://blogs.richardson.com/2013/01/11/top-needs-identified-by-b2b-sales-reps-for-success-in-2013/>.

Siegel, Daniel J. 1999. *The Developing Mind: How Relationships and the Brain Interact to Shape Who We Are*. New York, NY: The Guilford Press.

Skolnick, Ethan. "5 Reasons LeBron James Can Be Even Better in 2013-14." *The Bleacher Report*. 17 Sept 2013. <http://

bleacherreport.com/articles/1686060-5-reasons-lebron-james-can-be-even-better-in-2013-14>.

Spiro, Rosann L., and Barton A. Weitz. 1990. "Adaptive Selling: Conceptualization, Measurement, and Nomological Validity." *Journal of Marketing Research* 27.1: 61-69.

Thirteen, prod. "The Human Spark: Brain Matters." *The Human Spark: Brain Matters.* PBS. Arlington, VA, 20 Jan. 2010. Television.

Tracy, Brian. 2007. *The Psychology of Selling.* Nashville, TN: Thomas Nelson.

Wooden, John, and Jack Tobin. 1972. *They Call Me Coach.* Waco, TX: Word.

ABOUT THE AUTHOR

Sedric Hill has over twenty-five years of equity and in sales, sales management, leadership and coaching highlighted with a distinguished record of success including over 20 President's Club awards along with many other high honors and other accomplishments.

In 1985, Sedric began his career at McKesson Corporation where he developed the foundations of his selling philosophy: hard work plus superior skills applied to the right things, equals success. In 1987, Sedric met his business mentor, Ben Wiley, a former IBM top sales rep who founded his own of company: International Business Consumables (IBC). Sedric joined IBC where his selling and business skills grew quickly.

In 1992, Sedric joined Pitney Bowes, as a sales representative before working his way up to top management over a 17 year career. It was at here in 2003, where Sedric delivered one of his greatest successes with the company when he designed a unique training program for the western region's customer service department. The program, dubbed: Find the Mail, was designed to improve sales of complex software products. Because of the program's success, it was rolled out nationally to all software service technicians while generating over $100 million dollars in incremental revenue. In 2007, Sedric was appointed to lead a regional sales force within Pitney Bowes' newly acquired presort business. Through his leadership, the region went from worst to first in total revenue within the first 18 months.

In 2009, Sedric co-founded Sales Development & Performance, LLC (SD&P) in order to provide a platform to expand his work beyond a single corporation. SD&P initially worked with training organizations helping them improve their training impact and value to their clients. Here, Sedric began his research on selling expertise, for what would later become his first book: Expert Selling.

In 2010, Sedric joined Neopost where he drew from his in depth experience in sales and coaching to lead another team to success, achieving multiple president's club honors. Here, Sedric also expanded his interest in discovering the most influential aspects of business success–working closely with the top sales leaders within the company.

In 2013, Sedric returned to run SD&P full time. He reorganized the company's focus and grew it significantly by providing custom training, business consulting, and coaching services to sales forces, and individuals who depend on the use of persuasive communication. As a training and development entrepreneur, Sedric has introduced several new innovative concepts that are changing the paradigms in today's training; Video Interactive Practice™ (VIP) is a unique training approach specifically designed to advance expertise by enhancing traditional training. Sales Brain Trainers (SBTs) are interactive smartphone apps that enable users to target and improve mental selling skills anytime, anywhere. Performance-Based Learning™ (PBL) is a creative learning approach aimed at improving skill and performance through routine work. Each of these learning innovations are rooted in Expert-Based Training (XBT) science and related academic research.

If you are interested in working with SD&P for your training, coaching, or business advisory needs, contact Sedric at shill@sales-blueprint.com, or visit www.sales-blueprint.com. You can also hire Sedric as a keynote speaker at your next business event or sales meeting.